From the Jordan to Jerusalem, from Joshua to Solomon, YEARS OF DARKNESS, DAYS OF GLORY presents the enduring lessons from Israel's history.

Israel was once a world power, its rulers renowned for their wisdom, poetry, and warfare. But God had something more in mind for His people than place and power in the family of nations. His true purpose for Israel—and for you and me—can be found only in a deep and close personal relationship with Him. It is the presence of God . . . that is the true glory of God's people.

The glory that was Israel's in Solomon's time has faded now. Nothing remains. But the glory that will be Israel's when Jesus, David's greater Son, sits on the throne, and the glory that will be ours with Him, is still ahead.

YEARS OF DARKNESS, DAYS OF GLORY is a living story that reaches out to include all mankind in its vision of the glorious Kingdom of God.

LARRY RICHARDS
BIBLE ALIVE SERIES

Years of Darkness Days of Glory

Lessons from Israel's History

Studies in Joshua through the time of Solomon

David C. Cook Publishing Co.

ELGIN, ILLINOIS—WESTON, ONTARIO
LA HABRA, CALIFORNIA

ACKNOWLEDGMENT
Special acknowledgment is made for permission to reprint material from *A Survey of Israel's History* by Leon Wood. Copyright © 1970 Zondervan Publishing House.

YEARS OF DARKNESS, DAYS OF GLORY

David C. Cook Publishing Co., Elgin, IL 60120

Printed in the United States of America
ISBN: 0-912692-97-9

CONTENTS

YEARS OF DARKNESS, DAYS OF GLORY

THE ADVENTURE BEGINS

THE DIPLOMAT PACED THE FLOOR, wondering how to answer this latest dispatch from the East. How was he ever to sort out these conflicting reports! Which of the splinter parties really was loyal to his own nation? Was it the group in power now? Or were they just using the military and economic aid to feather their own nests? Of course they were corrupt, but would a different set of leaders prove any more effective? If he could only know which factions were under control of that other world power, then . . .

He continued pacing.

If only he could see some light at the end of the tunnel.

The man we're watching is no Washington diplomat concerned about Southeast Asia. He is an Egyptian diplomat, pacing in an office in the city of Akhetaten, about the time of the Hebrew conquest of Palestine. And it is Palestine, not Southeast Asia, that is his concern. Far to the north of Egypt, the last decades have seen the rise of a powerful rival empire—the Hittite. Egypt and the Hittites came into conflict when the Hittites removed parts of Syria and Phoenicia from Egyptian control.

Syria and Palestine had been in Egypt's sphere of influence for some time. But now in many of the smaller city-states a nationalistic fervor was growing. Eager to cast off the imperialistic yoke of Egypt's influence, local princes already hoping to rebel and gain independence were encouraged by the Hittites. Conflict between rebels and loyalists broke out. Both sides sent letters to Egypt affirming their loyalty and accusing the other. Often both sides had lobbyists in the Egyptian court to look after their interests. Confused by the conflicting reports and the intrigue, the Egyptian state department seemed unable to distinguish between its friends and its foes!

Soon the influence and the power of Egypt in Asia were sapped. Confused and uncertain, hesitant and indecisive, this once great world power, though still one of the strongest nations of the ancient world, lost her grip over her former territories.

THE AMARNA LETTERS

This day in history, which sounds all too much like our own, is well-known today because of the recovery of diplomatic correspondence between Egyptian government officials and various groups in Syria and Palestine. The ruins of Akhetaton, known now as Tell el-Amarna, have given up some 400 letters (written on clay tablets) since the first accidental discovery in 1887. In them, we get a revealing picture of an area which included the land that God's people, under the leadership of Joshua, were about to conquer.

In earlier books of this series (*Let Day Begin, Freedom Road*), we have traced Bible history from Creation to the Exodus. In Genesis, we saw God choose Abraham and give him covenant promises (Gen. 12, 15, 17). The Abrahamic Covenant was God's announcement of His purposes in our world. Abraham would have a host of descendants, some of whom would be formed into a special people (the Jews) through whom God would work out His plan. God promised Abraham He would set aside the land of Palestine for this people. Through this people God promised, looking forward to the Messiah (Christ), that "all the peoples of the earth" would be blessed.

The rest of Genesis tells the story of the line through which the promises would be fulfilled— Isaac, Abraham's son, and Jacob (later renamed Israel), Abraham's grandson. Genesis also tells how God providentially sent Joseph, one of Israel's twelve sons, down into Egypt to prepare that land for a coming famine and to prepare a place for the family of Israel to stay.

As we trace the history of the Israelites beyond

11

the Book of Genesis, we see that the chosen people lived on in Egypt for more than 400 years! After a time they were enslaved, and for decades experienced great hardship. Finally God sent a specially prepared leader, Moses, to bring Israel out of servitude and to lead this now great people to the land promised to Abraham.

Deliverance from Egypt was accomplished only by direct and miraculous divine intervention. God brought a series of plagues on Egypt in judgment. Finally Pharaoh, the ruler of Egypt, did release Israel—only to change his mind and pursue them with an army. The army itself was destroyed at the Yam Suf (The Reed or Red Sea),[1] which opened to permit the Israelites to cross and then rushed together to drown the Egyptians. Rejoicing, the now freed slaves moved out into the wilderness!

But centuries of servitude had weakened the fiber of the people. They consistently resisted and rejected God and Moses' leadership. As an aid to discipline, and to reveal God's moral character and expectations for His people, the Israelites were led to Mount Sinai. There the Law was given. The people were promised that while disobedience would bring discipline and disappointment, obedience would lead to blessing. Israel willingly accepted God's standards and promised to obey.

But Israel's promise was too lightly made. In

---

[1]*Yam Suf* is a transliteration of the Hebrew name for the body of water. The exact identification is uncertain, but most scholars feel that it was one of the lakes in the area of the Suez Canal and not the Red Sea itself. See a good commentary for discussion of the issue.

12

fact, disobedience continued to distinguish the people who came out of Egypt with Moses. This disobedience reached a climax when the nation, poised on the border of the Promised Land, was commanded to go in. Moses sent twelve spies into the land to survey it and report. Ten of them came back terrified by the strength of the fortified cities and the stature of the inhabitants. Only two, Joshua and Caleb, came back enthusiastic, confident that God would give them the land. Characteristically, the people of Israel listened to the ten and doubted God. All the urging of Moses and Aaron and the insistence of Joshua and Caleb that they were able to take the land went for nothing. The people refused to obey God's command.

Israel had made a basic choice. Because the people would not trust God or obey Him, that generation could not enter the Promised Land. God forced them back out into the wilderness. There the people of Israel wandered for 38 years, until the entire generation of adults who had refused to trust God had died in the wilderness. All but Joshua and Caleb. These two men of faith survived, and over the years the old generation was replaced by a new one.

The new generation grew up with a greater trust in God. Tested in battle, they obeyed. Finally, as the Book of Deuteronomy describes, the new generation was once again camped outside the Promised Land, awaiting God's command to cross over the Jordan and take their inheritance. In his last act as their leader, Moses reviewed the love of God

13

for His people and urged the new generation to keep His Law. This generation also stood up to accept the standard of the Law and to promise obedience to the Lord. This time the promise was not made lightly. The discipline of the previous years had produced a committed band.

With the death of Moses and the appointment of Joshua to lead God's people on to victory, the adventure recorded in the Book of Joshua begins.

And the Amarna letters? They tell us that God had quietly been at work, preparing the stage for Israel's adventure!

During much of the 400 years that Israel was in Egypt, Palestine served as a land bridge between Egypt and a succession of world powers to the north, as well as their battleground. The people of Israel, who had multiplied from the seventy[2] some men and women who entered Egypt to more than two million, could never have increased to such great numbers if God had left them in the Promised Land. Then, at just the time when Israel was ready to enter that land, the influence of Egypt had waned in Palestine! In the power vacuum which existed—into a land divided into petty kingdoms—God's people moved, ready to overcome a people numerically greater than themselves.

Even as today diplomatic success and failure serve only to further the outworking of God's plans, so it was in Bible times.

[2]This number counts only the direct descendants of Jacob. See Gen. 46: 26, 27.

It's important to keep this in mind. So often when we read the Bible we think of the people and events described as distant or unreal. But the Egyptian diplomat in one of the luxuriously decorated brick buildings of Akhetaton who puzzled over the complex world situation is not so different from the State Department undersecretary in modern Washington. Their problems would be much the same. At night each would return to a suburban home, passing crowded and disorganized clusters of apartment houses. Cocktail parties and political maneuvering (if not between Republican and Democrat, then between the Amon priesthood party and the party of Pharaoh) shaped the life-style then as now.

And even as emerging nations struggle today to establish their existence, so in Palestine the people of Israel were about to emerge as a nation and to challenge a people long established.

How real it all is! Just as real, just as living, as today's current events.

But what took place then has a unique timelessness. Events occurring in Washington today affect us and our future. But so do the events of Scripture which we're about to study! In the people and events described in God's Word, you and I discover timeless truths about ourselves and our relationship with God. The Bible's word of history becomes, by the activity of the Holy Spirit, God's voice guiding us today. As we listen, learn, and respond to the one who speaks to us through the reality of our heritage's sacred past, you and I can

15

see our own years of darkness fade away and welcome the days of glory God intends to unfold. Opening the Word to Joshua is both to revisit living history and to open up our own lives to learn from God today. We turn in our Bibles to a page on which a great adventure is about to begin. For Israel—and for you and me as well.

FOUNDATION FOR CONQUEST
Joshua 1–8

The Book of Joshua opens with the phrase "after the death of Moses." There is a great transition here, the kind of transition that comes when a young person leaves the family and starts off on his own. Or when a marriage takes place, and the young couple leave their fathers and mothers to establish a new home.

For some eighty years—and for four entire books of the Old Testament—the man Moses had been the dominant figure. But now Israel had to strike out and face the challenge of the future without him.

It's helpful to look at these early chapters of Joshua and discover the resources God provides for His adventuring people.

An equipped leader (Josh. 1). God does not want a leaderless people. But He wants leaders who are uniquely equipped.

Joshua's previous experience had prepared him for leadership. He had earlier led the Israelite defense against an attack by the Amalekites (Ex.

16

17: 8-16), indicating previous battlefield experience. It is likely that he had served in the Egyptian army prior to the Exodus; foreigners were often enlisted in the military services. As one of the twelve spies, Joshua had learned firsthand the topography of Palestine. At that time his trust in God had led him to advise immediate attack when all the other spies but Caleb urged the people to disobey. Joshua's character matched his experience. Later, at God's direction, he was invested with some of Moses' authority (Num. 27: 20).

Usually the road to significant leadership is a long one, with many choices along the way. What you and I do with our less significant opportunities determines the part we'll play.

It was not simply character and experience that equipped Joshua for leadership. This first chapter of the book bearing his name makes it clear that the leader's relationship with God is critical. Joshua had basic spiritual resources that are ours as well. How Joshua used the divine resources would make the difference between victory and defeat. What were his resources?

(1) Joshua had the promise of God's purpose. "Every place that the sole of your foot shall tread upon, that have I given unto you" (Josh. 1: 3). God's announced purpose was to give Israel the Promised Land.

(2) Joshua had the promise of God's presence. "As I was with Moses, so I will be with thee: I will not fail thee, nor forsake thee" (Josh. 1: 5). God committed Himself to be with His servant and to

take on Himself the burden of success.

(3) Joshua had the promise of God's faithfulness. "You shall cause this people to inherit the land which I swore to their fathers to give them" (Josh. 1: 6, RSV). God had committed Himself to a cause, and He would not let His promise fail.

Against this expression of commitment by God there was one requirement made of Joshua: "Only be thou strong and very courageous, that thou mayest observe to do according to all the law, which Moses my servant commanded thee" (Josh. 1: 7). Neither discouragement nor fear were to influence Joshua to hesitate or to disobey. If Joshua would live in close relationship to the Lord, being responsive and obedient to Him, victory was assured. *The leader is to be a man who follows God.*

The emphasis in this first chapter on the vital role of obedience is repeated, not only in Joshua and in the Book of Judges which follows, but throughout the section of Scripture we will be studying. Every event, every individual, reflects the basic principle: obedience brings victory; disobedience brings defeat.

We see the lesson first taught in the battles of Jericho and Ai. We see the lesson taught again and again through the days of the judges. And we see it repeated in individuals like David and Saul. Responsiveness to God, the willingness to live as He directs and to stay in close fellowship with Him, is not only a prerequisite for leadership. It is a prerequisite for any blessing. Then. And now.

First steps (Josh. 3, 4). The Jordan River was in

flood stage, blocking Israel from Palestine. These chapters tell how God began to demonstrate that he was with Joshua and the people. The flow of water stopped and the people crossed on dry ground. Israel recognized Joshua as one who was following God's directions (3: 7, 8), and they in turn willingly followed him.

There would be many more opportunities for God to demonstrate His faithfulness and presence. But this early evidence was important for Israel's morale and to help them trust in Joshua's leadership.

Jericho–point (Josh. 2, 5, 6). I noted earlier that the principle demonstrated over and over again now in Israel's experience is stated in Joshua 1. "Be careful to do according to all that is written in [the book of the Law] . . . for then you shall . . . have good success" (Josh. 1: 8, RSV). Obedience will bring victory. Invariably.

Note that it is not belief that brings success.

Joshua 2 tells of two spies who visited the walled city of Jericho, which controls the passes leading to the interior of Palestine. There they met a prostitute named Rahab, and were hidden by her from the city authorities. Rahab told the spies that everyone in the city had heard of Israel's God and knew how He had dried up the sea and brought them military victories. These pagan people believed the report! "As soon as we had heard these things," Rahab related, "our hearts did melt, neither did there remain any more courage in any man, because of you: for the Lord your God, he is

19

God in heaven above, and in earth beneath" (Josh. 2:11).

But what was the reaction of those who heard and believed? They shut up their city and hid behind the walls—and tried to catch and kill the Israelites who came to spy. Their belief did not lead them to turn to God; in fact, it hardened them in their resistance!

How different with Rahab. She believed enough to commit herself to take sides with God. She acted on her belief—she helped the spies escape and trusted herself to the Lord and His people. It was belief translated by action into trust which marked Rahab off from the other inhabitants of Jericho.

Chapters 5 and 6 show that trust, expressed as obedience, is also taught in Israel's victory over Jericho. Just before the battle, Joshua reconnoiters Jericho and is met by a figure holding a drawn sword. This figure announces himself to be "captain of the host of the Lord" (Josh. 5:14). Joshua's response is to bow down and await orders.

From a military standpoint, the orders given are ridiculous. Joshua is to march the people of Israel around the city of Jericho once a day for six days. On these circuits no one is to make a sound. On the seventh day, seven circuits are to be made. Then, at a signal, all the people are to shout. And, so the promise goes, when the people shout, the walls of the city will fall down. Israel then is to attack and utterly destroy the city, saving only those in Rahab's house. Nothing is to be salvaged, and no booty taken. All is to be destroyed.

However foolish Israel may have felt during those seven days, they did obey. Whatever uncertainty Joshua may have experienced, he was strong enough to do as he had been commanded.

On the seventh day, when the people shouted with a great shout, the walls did come tumbling down.

It is this kind of belief, which expresses itself in obedience, which is the "trust" God calls us all to have in Him.

Ai—counterpoint (Josh. 7, 8). At Jericho one of the Hebrew warriors, a man named Achan, disobeyed God's command and took gold and silver. This hidden sin led to Israel's defeat at the minor city of Ai. Sin had broken fellowship with God; the flow of promised power was interrupted.

Achan was sought out and he and his family stoned. Their disobedience had led to the death of 36 men of Israel in the battle of Ai, and the defeat could potentially rally the surrounding enemy to attack Israel. But when sin was dealt with, Ai was taken in a second attempt and, like Jericho, totally destroyed. A graphic lesson had been taught. Obedience to God was vital after all. Obedience brought victory; disobedience resulted in disastrous defeat.

With both these lessons deeply impressed, Israel then stood as Joshua read the whole of the divine Law. The way of blessing and the way of curse were laid out before them all. And so, with God's guiding truth again attuned, the great adventure had begun.

GOING DEEPER

Each chapter of this book will orient you to the content of a particular section of the Old Testament. These *Going Deeper* suggestions at the end of each chapter are to guide you in reading from that section of the Bible itself, and will help you probe Scripture's personal meaning for you today.

to personalize

1. Read Joshua 1. What parallels do you think exist between Joshua's "equipment" and your own? How does this section apply to believers today?

2. Examine the story of Jericho (Josh. 2, 5, 6). From these chapters develop several examples of the impact of belief vs. trust. What do you think God intended His people to learn from these experiences? What is He teaching us?

3. The story of Achan's sin and the defeat at Ai has raised a number of questions. How would you answer these typical ones? (a) Why did Israel have to be defeated because of one man's sin? (b) Why was Achan's family killed with him (see 7:21 for one possibility)? (c) Why did God insist on the total destruction of Jericho in the first place? Isn't this "brutality" out of character for Him?

to probe

1. What can you find out from archaeological sources about the Amarna letters and about the excavations of Jericho?

2. Develop a character sketch of Joshua, drawing on references in Exodus through Deuteronomy which you locate with a concordance.

3. Write a one-page exploration of the meaning for believers today of any one of these eight chapters.

AT REST

THE STORY OF THE BOOK OF JOSHUA is not so much a record of conquest as a report of entrance into rest. There are adventures aplenty! But the thrust of the book is summed up in these words: "And they possessed it [the land], and dwelt therein. And the Lord gave them rest round about, according to all that he sware unto their fathers . . . There failed not ought of any good thing which the Lord had spoken unto the house of Israel; all came to pass" (21: 43-45).

You and I might be tempted to dwell on the adventures of the conquest. Instead, God focuses our attention on achieving the goal of rest.

THE CONQUEST
Joshua 9–13

After the transjordan nations (across the Jordan River from Palestine) had been conquered,

Joshua's campaign began with an attack on Jericho. This key city, just above the Israelite base of Gilgal, gave access both to the heart of Palestine and to Joshua's source of supply across the Jordan. It also controlled two trade routes up into the central highlands. In taking Ai and Bethel (8: 17; 12: 16) Joshua cut the land in two and was then able to plan and campaign against a divided enemy, dealing first with the southern and then with the northern kings.

The taking of Jericho first was thus of great strategic importance. And here divine intervention seemed essential. Leon Wood in *A Survey of Israel's History* describes Jericho's walls:

[They] were of a type which made direct assault practically impossible. An approaching enemy first encountered a stone abutment, eleven feet high, back and up from which sloped a 35 degree plastered scarp reaching to the main wall some 35 vertical feet above. The steep smooth slope prohibited battering the wall by any effective device or building fires to break it. An army trying to storm the wall found difficulty in climbing the slope, and ladders to scale it would find no satisfactory footing. The normal tactic used by an army to take a city so protected was siege, but Israel did not have time for this, if she was to occupy all the land in any reasonable number of months.

Any impression we may have that Palestine was some rustic backwater and that Joshua's army was like some overwhelming hoard of savages is quickly dispelled by such a description. The men of Palestine were acquainted with war; their offensive and defensive skills were highly sophisticated! But they had no defense against Israel's God. Jericho's walls, which normally would have held off Israel for months or even years, fell down in a moment.

While God's power did provide victory in times of crisis, Joshua usually employed field tactics to defeat his enemy. Surprise attacks, forced marches, and flying columns which dashed ahead to cut off lines of retreat were all tactics known by Hittite commanders of that day and used brilliantly by Joshua. As in Israel's recent Six-Day War with the Arab states, Israel by aggressive tactics defeated an enemy with forces much stronger than their own.

The purpose of Joshua's campaign was not to destroy all peoples living in Palestine, but rather to eliminate all effective opposition. The power of the Palestinian people to threaten the existence of Israel was to be crushed. Thus Joshua did not concentrate on the conquest of land but the defeat of enemy armies. Some of the cities against which the Israelites fought were taken and their population destroyed. But other cities were not burned. Later those unrazed cities were reoccupied by survivors. However, the principal cities were "devoted" to God; they and their entire populations were completely destroyed.

Questions about the Conquest. Commentators have

been universally impressed with Joshua's military strategy. In fact, the Israeli War College today features a study of his campaigns! But two questions about these early chapters of Joshua are consistently raised.

(1) *The long day (Josh. 10:12-14).* Israel made a surprise attack on an army gathered by five southern kings. The enemy was routed and fled. During their panicked rout the enemy soldiers were struck down by great hailstones falling from the sky as well as by Joshua's men. Determined to crush their enemies before they could reach the safety of their walled cities, Joshua cried out, "Sun, stand thou still upon Gibeon; and thou, Moon, in the valley of Ajalon" (vs. 12). The Biblical text reports, "The sun stood still, and the moon stayed" (vs. 13).

Some have suggested that what happened here was a miracle involving refraction of light. The day was *apparently* lengthened. Others have argued that the request really was for the sun to "be silent," that is, to stop shining so strongly that its heat would sap the strength of the pursuing Israelites. However, the language of the text, and particularly the statement that this day was unique and twice the normal length between noon and sunset, seems to indicate that the day was miraculously prolonged.

(2) *Total destruction.* The ruthlessness with which Israel dealt with the Canaanites has raised a theological question, since the extermination was done at God's express command (Deut. 7:1-5; 20:16-18; Josh. 11:20). How can this be recon-

28

ciled with the New Testament picture of a God of love?

Materially and culturally the Canaanites had an advanced civilization. Archaeology has shown well-planned cities with homes of good design and construction. Drainage systems had been installed, trade was carried on with distant countries, skilled workmanship was shown in metals and pottery. But for all the cultural advancement, the Palestinian religious and moral life had shown great decline.

When Abraham lived in Palestine there was no developed cult of Baal (a nature and fertility god). But over the centuries the worship of Baal and his female counterpart had come to dominate Canaan, and with this worship had come a host of associated immoral practices described in Leviticus 18. The sentence of destruction was passed to protect Israel from contamination by the surrounding peoples.

But it is also important to realize that the Canaanites were not destroyed out of hand. In Abraham's day there had been some knowledge of God in the land (see Gen. 14: 17-20). In fact, God refused to dispossess the Canaanites in Abraham's time "for the iniquity of the Amorites is not yet full" (Gen. 15: 16).

We must look at the events of the Conquest in the light of divine judgment on sin. God did not command Joshua to destroy an innocent people. God chose to use Israel as the means by which He brought a well-deserved judgement upon one of

29

the most immoral cultures of the civilized world. And even within that context, those like Rahab who would turn to God could hope for deliverance.

And so within a number of months the army of the Lord completed the rout of the enemy and was ready to take its rest.

THE LAND DIVIDED
Joshua 13-22

The majority of the Book of Joshua describes not the conquest but the distribution of their inheritance to the twelve tribes of Israel. Large portions of territory were blocked out and the different tribes told to possess their land. This often meant continuing to battle with Canaanites who still lived there. The power to resist Israel in a massive way had been destroyed in Joshua's campaign. Yet pockets of resistance were still found in each tribe's allotment. These mopping-up operations would keep God's people dependent on Him—and make sure that they did not lose their skill in war.

With the victory won, the fighting men of those tribes which had settled across the Jordan but had come into the land with their brothers to help them fight their battles could return home. Throughout the occupied land of Palestine the victorious Hebrews began to enjoy the rest which God had promised and which through His faithfulness had now come true.

FIGURE I   **PALESTINE AT THE CONQUEST**

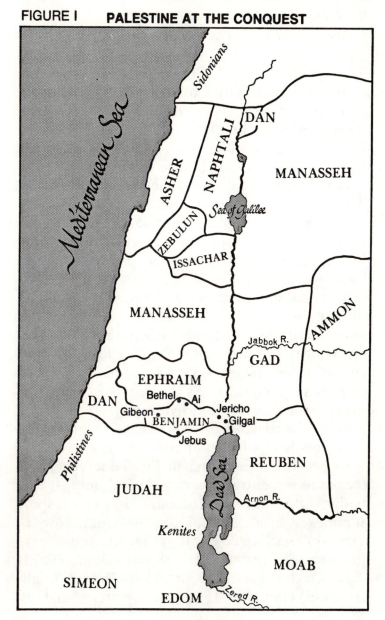

REST'S LIFE-STYLE
Joshua 20, 21

These chapters tell of the establishment of cities of refuge and of cities for the Levites within the allotments of the other tribes. These provisions remind us that the people of Israel were now to begin a life-style which was carefully planned and revealed by God long before the Conquest.

If you've studied the earlier books of the Old Testament, you're familiar with God's careful definition of His people's life-style. This definition included not only moral and religious injunctions; it also carefully structured every aspect of the new society.

The case law chapters (Ex. 20—24) spelled out a number of specific implications the Ten Commandments had for Israel's life in the land. Commitment to the love of God and to love for one's neighbor was to mark God's people as His own distinctive possession. As the people of Israel followed God's laws for holy living, poverty, injustice, and all the social ills which warp human society could be dealt with compassionately.

In the life-style sketched by divine revelation there was no central government or administrative bodies. Obedience was to God. Elders had responsibilities in local communities. As Wood notes (*A Survey of Israel's History*), they "served as judges of persons who had killed someone (Deut. 19:12), conducted inquests (Deut. 21:2), heard family problems (Deut. 21:18f), settled matrimonial disputes (Deut. 22:15; 25:7), and settled cases of controversy at the gate of the city (Ruth 4:2)."

Local courts shared cases with the elders, and when a case could not be settled, it was sent to the central sanctuary in Shiloh. There, before the Tabernacle of the Lord, a court of priests and lay judges made a final and binding determination.

The Tabernacle, which had been built to God's specifications and remained the symbol of God's presence with Israel, was now the great unifying center of Israel's life. Here the sacrifices commanded by God were made, and no sacrifices were to be made at any other location. Three times a year every healthy male citizen was to gather here for the feasts around which the worship and religious life of Israel centered.

The first of these feasts was the Passover (Ex. 12:1-13; Deut. 16:1-8), which began the religious year and commemorated God's deliverance of His people from Egypt. For fourteen days the people gathered (in April) to renew and reaffirm their commitment to the God of the Exodus.

At the close of the wheat harvest some 50 days later, a one-day observation (called the Feast of Weeks, see Ex. 23:16; Lev. 23:15-22; Num. 28:26-31; Deut. 16:9-12) was held.

The third feast was a week-long commemoration in September-October of Israel's life in the wilderness. Families lived in tents or booths outside, and the occasion was called the Feast of Tabernacles (Ex. 23:16; Lev. 23:34-43; Deut. 16:13-15).

These three feasts were not, however, the only way in which the unity of the twelve tribes was maintained. There were other feasts they had in common, and all the tribes kept the Sabbath as a day of rest. Common customs and common laws, with a common language and history, bound Israel together as a larger family of God.

The common custom is well illustrated by the cities of refuge established by Joshua in obedience to God's earlier command through Moses. In Israel, a murderer was to be put to death. This sentence—already passed by God on one who killed another—was to be executed by a relative of the murdered man, "the avenger of blood" (Josh. 20:5).

But the Old Testament recognized an important distinction between premeditated murder and accidental death. The murderer was to be executed without fail. But one guilty of manslaughter was permitted to flee to a city of refuge. There he lived until the death of the high priest, after which he could return to his home without fear of retribution. There were six such cities scattered throughout the territories of the twelve tribes. These cities were the common possession of the whole people.

The common law is represented by the establishment of Levitical cities through the land. When God established the Tabernacle worship system, He set aside the family of Levi to serve Him. The descendants of Aaron served as priests; descendants of the other family members were singers, caretakers, and teachers. The role of teacher is particularly significant when we see the Levitical cities placed in the allotments of the other tribes. Only the tribe of Levi did not receive its own territory. God was its portion. But they did live among the others, with men from the Levitical cities taking their turn at serving in the central sanctuary. Taught there, they returned to serve as teachers of the Law throughout Israel.

The tribes of Israel retained their separate identity and were directly responsible to God rather than to a central human authority. But the lifestyle God established for them constantly reaffirmed their unity as the special people of God and provided for continuous instruction in His ways.

The structure of early Israel, so briefly described here, was a theocracy—a government where God is the head of state. In Israel's case, God was the "Great King." The tragedy of Israel is that she did not continue in obedient relationship to God. Israel abandoned rest's life-style. The society broke down. Social injustice, poverty, unrest, conflict, fear, and pain all followed.

In God's Church today, as in early Israel, our rest and peace depend on committing ourselves to trust in God—and to obedience.

JOSHUA'S DEATH
Joshua 23, 24

Joshua had led Israel to victory and guided them in establishing the theocratic society. In these concluding chapters, Joshua looked back, and he also looked ahead. In view of all that God has done for Israel, Joshua demanded total commitment. "Now therefore fear the Lord, and serve him in sincerity and in truth" (24:14).

Standing before this venerable saint who had led them to experience God's rest, the people reaffirmed their commitment to obey. And the Biblical record echoes that commitment: "And Israel served the Lord all the days of Joshua, and all the days of the elders that overlived Joshua, and which had known all the works of the Lord, that he had done for Israel" (24:31).

Obedience to God had won them rest.

GOING DEEPER
to personalize

1. Begin your exploration of these chapters by reading the following sections:
   a) Joshua 11:16-23. This is the summary of the campaign of conquest.
   b) Joshua 14. Here is what happened to Caleb, one of the two spies who had been willing to attack Canaan some 40 years before.
   c) Joshua 17. Read this for a picture of the challenge still awaiting individual tribes, even after the power of the Canaanite kings had been broken.
   d) Joshua 23, 24. You'll really want to visit the aged Joshua and get his personal impressions of Israel's past—and its future.
2. Several incidents deserve more careful study,

because they have fascinating application to us today. Pick one of the two following passages and do some in-depth thinking about the Biblical record and its implications for you. The questions included are simply starter questions. You'll want to add your own as you explore.

a) *The Gibeonites.* Joshua 9 tells of a trick that preserved this people from destruction. How did they get away with it? Why was a bargain, struck under false pretenses, kept by Israel? (Note Ps. 15: 1, 4 for some insight.) What does Joshua's behavior here tell us about his concept of God? (What do our actions tell about our concept of God?)

b) *Reuben and Gad.* Joshua 22 tells of the return of these tribes to their Transjordan possessions. On the way they stopped to build an altar—and suddenly found themselves on the verge of war with the other tribes! Why was war threatened? What was the motivation of the ten tribes? How does their action demonstrate the kind of commitment that is necessary to make a theocracy work? And, how was war avoided?

to probe

1. It is particularly significant that the theocratic structure of Israel when it entered the land stressed communication within the tribes (the feasts, the placement of the Levitical cities) and decentralized authority. Control was to be exer-

cised by God through His Law, not by a human being or human agency. This particular structure was functional as long as people and communities were committed to the divine life-style.

Examine then, in a five-page paper, parallels between the theocratic structure of Israel and the Church. What does it really mean that Christ is Head of His body the Church? Is the Church to function as a theocratic community? If so, how can this structure work? And, how do our Church organizations today reflect—or reject—the divine life-style?

2. From the Book of Deuteronomy, reconstruct as complete a picture as possible of the life-style Israel was to display in the Promised Land. Point by point, discuss parallels or contrasts with the Christian's life-style today.

PART I

YEARS
OF DARKNESS

INTRODUCTION

Moses' last words to Israel before sending them on to conquer and find rest were these: "The Lord thy God will set thee on high above all nations of the earth: And all these blessings shall come on thee, and overtake thee" (Deut. 28:1, 2). Under Joshua, the nation knew just such exaltation.

But after the death of Joshua's generation, a process of deterioration set in. Instead of the blessings promised, Israel began to experience defeat. Instead of possessing the land, they were pushed back by their neighbors. Instead of being feared, they were afraid.

Why? What happened to the blessing?

The Biblical record makes it clear. Israel neglected the one condition for blessing. Blessing was ordained only "if you obey the voice of the Lord your God, being careful to do all his commandments" (Deut. 28:1, RSV). The years of darkness were directly related to Israel's neglect of that trust in God which frees man to obey.

WHEN JUDGES RULED

GLANCING THROUGH any high school yearbook, you can see them. Old pictures, young faces, class prophecies—and one person voted by his classmates "most likely to succeed." All too often the prophecy is wrong. The passage of years saps the strength of the promise; the idealistic confidence of youth is replaced by tired realism.

It's often like this for Christians. In the early bloom of faith, we look ahead with eagerness to all we'll do for God. "Another Paul," we think. Or another Billy Graham. Or at least some lesser hero of the faith. But all too often the years sap that promise. And we, too, settle down for something less than that for which we had dreamed—and hoped—and prayed.

Israel, just entering her rest after the Conquest, might well have been voted "most likely to succeed" by the surrounding nations who feared her.

Deep within, her own dreams must have stirred, dreams quickened by the promise implicit in her relationship with God: "And all people of the earth shall see that thou art called by the name of the Lord" (Deut. 28:10). In the failure of Israel to fulfill her potential, God warns future generations of His people. He gives each of us a very special invitation: an invitation to walk steadfastly (or to return to) the pathway to blessing which Israel forsook.

DRIFTING FROM REST
Judges 1:1–3:6

The Book of Judges begins with an overview and ends with a summary. The first chapters of this book provide a brief analysis of why Israel's great promise was never realized. The middle section (3:7—16:31) traces chronologically the history of the judges and the conditions of their times. The final section summarizes and, through two case histories, vividly demonstrates the results of Israel's choice to abandon God's ways.

The key to understanding the decline recorded here is found in Judges 2:10: "There arose

FIGURE II **THE BOOK OF JUDGES**

Causes	Conditions		Consequences	
1 - 3	3	- 16	17	- 21

another generation after them [Joshua's generation], which knew not the Lord, nor yet the works which he had done for Israel." Israel's rest and blessing were dependent on obedience to God. But obedience in turn hinged on knowing the Lord—well.

The New Testament picks up this same theme. "Whoever has my commands and obeys them, he is the one who loves me" (Jn. 14:21, *New International Version*). Obedience to God will result from relationship and be dependent on love. We do not coolly choose to obey in order to gain God's affection. It is only when we know that we are loved by God, and when we love Him in return, that love and trust awaken in us the capacity to obey.

The new generation, in drifting away from a personal relationship with God, inevitably lost the capacity to trust Him and to obey. Rest and blessing, contingent on living out the Law's life-style, were inevitably lost as well.

These early chapters of Judges trace Israel's breakdown and record a revealing progression.

Incomplete obedience. Joshua had broken the ability of the Canaanites to organize resistance against Israel. Then the land had been divided among the tribes, and each tribe commanded to clear its own territory.

Archaeological evidence combines with the biblical record to indicate that Israel was successful in the hills of Palestine but not in the low-lying areas. The power of the remaining peoples was concentrated in the lowlands, and the Canaanites had adopted chariot warfare. Unable to cope with these chariots of iron, the tribes involved failed to drive the inhabitants out (Jdg. 1:31, 34). Even more serious, when Israel was victorious they chose not to drive them out! "When Israel grew strong," the author of Judges notes, "they put the Canaanites to forced labor, but did not utterly drive them out" (Jdg. 1:28, RSV; see vss. 30, 33, 35). The people of Israel valued slaves more than their covenant promise to the Lord!

God warned against this alarming tendency. Judges 2:1-5 tells of God's angel speaking to all the people of Israel. He reminded them that the Lord had made a firm covenant with Israel and had kept His word in bringing them into the Promised Land. Then came the rebuke: "I said . . . ye shall make no league with the inhabitants of this land; ye shall throw down their altars: but ye have not obeyed my voice: why have ye done this? Wherefore I also said, I will not drive them out from before you; but they shall be as thorns in your sides, and their gods shall be a snare unto you."

Apostasy. The wisdom of God in demanding that the Canaanites be driven out was demonstrated in what then happened. Influenced by the nature and fertility gods of the surrounding peoples, which appealed to the materialistic and sensual in their humanity, the Israelites "followed other gods . . . and bowed themselves unto them . . . they forsook the Lord, and served Baal and Ashtaroth" (2:12, 13).

Intermarriage. A third aspect of Israel's departure from God is seen in intermarriage (3: 5, 6). In this they not only denied their identity as a distinct and peculiar people of God, but also were further motivated to serve the pagan gods. The distinctive life-style defined in the Law, which was intended to reflect and to reveal the moral character of God, was rejected in favor of the immoral life-style of the people of the land. Israel denied her heritage, her identity, and her God.

THE SEVEN SINFUL CYCLES
Judges 3: 7–16: 31

In these chapters the Book of Judges gives a chronological survey of events during the centuries of darkness which followed for Israel. God's word had been abandoned and He Himself forsaken. The lesson the earlier generation had learned at Ai, the people of Israel now had to be taught again and again and again. This time, instead of involving a single family, the pattern of sin and subsequent judgment would sweep over the nation as a whole!

And there was a pattern. Seven repeated cycles of events are reported. First the Scriptural account reports that Israel fell into sin. As a result of sin, God brought judgment through the nearby nations, and God's people were forced into servitude. When the pressures became unbearable, Israel turned from her sin and cried out to God for deliverance. God heard Israel's prayers and a charismatic leader emerged to lead Israel—first to

FIGURE III

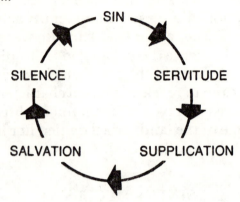

victory over the enemy and then morally, as a judge. During the leader's life the people knew a time of quiet and rest from oppression. But all too soon, they slipped back into the sinful ways of the pagans around them. With their fall into sin, the cycle had begun all over again!

Intensified. It is important to note, however, that with each cycle Israel appeared to become worse. Each subsequent judge had less impact until, with Samson, the judge himself was caught up in the very sins God called such leaders to restrain! So Samson found himself unable to bring rest to his people, even though he was militarily the most powerful of them all!

The chronology. The length of time the judges are said to have ruled adds up to 410 years. The actual period was probably about 335 years, since the time from Joshua's generation to the fourth year of Solomon (I Ki. 6: 1) is itself about 410 years. The reason for the discrepancy between the actual and

FIGURE IV — LIST OF THE JUDGES

NAME	OPPRESSORS	YEARS OF OPPRESSION AND REST	REFERENCE
Othniel	Mesopotamians	48	3:7-11
Ehud	Moabites	98	3:12-30
Shamgar			3:31
Deborah/Barak	Canaanites	60	4, 5
Gideon	Midianites	47	6-8
Tola		23	10:1, 2
Jair		22	10:3-5
Jephthah	Ammonites	24	10:6—12:7
Ibzan		7	12:8-10
Elon		10	12:11, 12
Abdon		8	12:13-15
Samson	Philistines	60†	13-16
TOTAL		407*	

†Some scholars would have Samson's 20 years running concurrently with the Philistines' 40 years.

*Abimelech, not a judge but a son of Gideon who set himself up as a king, ruled for three years (9:22) to bring the total number of years in the period to 410.

the apparent time span is that the ministry of the judges overlapped to some extent (see Jdg. 10: 7 and 3: 30—4: 1). The various oppressors were not the world powers of the day, but the neighbors Israel had failed to drive out. One judge might have been occupied with a people to the east at the same time another judge was occupied with the peoples to the west. Thus, we can't tell from internal chronology alone just how long the time was.

The judges. Twelve names are generally associated with the ministry of the judges. For most of them the calling was both military and civil. A judge emerged (was "raised up" by God, Jdg. 3: 9, 15, etc.) in time of need, led Israel in throwing off an enemy yoke, and then usually continued as a supervisor of God's people. The judges tried legal cases, and apparently most were successful in keeping the people from idolatry.

There was no office of "judge" prescribed in the Law. Yet it's clear that God sent these deliverers and gave at least four of them special enablement by His Spirit (3: 10; 6: 34; 11: 29; 15: 14).

The Philistines. These warlike people had come to the south coast of Palestine, possibly from Crete, but certainly from the Aegean area. During the years 1200 to 1000 B.C. (part of the time of the judges and during Saul's and David's reigns) they were the principal enemy of Israel. Five key cities (Ashkelon, Gaza, Ashdod, Gath, and Ekron) controlled both land and sea trade routes, making the territory the Philistines occupied wealthy and highly desirable.

48

The Philistine society, in contrast to the tribal structure of Israel, was highly organized. These people knew the secret of making and maintaining iron weapons. This gave them a military advantage over Israel, which lacked both a source for iron ore and the technology to work it. Ultimately the Philistines were able to establish garrisons at strategic points within Israel, and by the end of the period of the judges they had clearly embarked on a campaign to conquer the whole land.

Not until the time of David was this bitter enemy subdued. David reduced them to insignificance.

Thus these people, met here in Judges, play an increasingly significant role in the Biblical books which follow.

JUDGES FOR TODAY

Judges is the source of some of our most familiar Old Testament stories. The youngest children have heard tales of Samson and Gideon—over and over again. In fact, the very familiarity of stories from this book makes it likely that we'll miss its message!

As in all of Scripture, God communicates His message to men in the selection and recounting of events as well as in explicit teaching. As we listen and respond to what God says, the message of the written Word becomes an adventure with the living Word—Christ Himself. The written Word of God is the avenue through which God comes to us and invites us to enter into an ever-deepening personal relationship with Him.

Thus, it is dangerous to treat familiar portions of the Bible simply as stories. All too soon "Bible stories" take on a misty familiarity associated with our childhood—with the Mother Goose fantasy that captured our imagination then. But the stories of the Bible are not fantasy; they are the rugged fleshing out of reality. They are a living and powerful word to us from God, designed to captivate us as children—and to challenge us as adults. We need to take an adult look at this portion of God's Word and not rely on childhood impressions.

When we do examine Judges with our hearts tuned to respond to God's Word, we find a powerful message indeed. Along with the demonstration of the basic theme (Ai, now magnified and repeated over and over again), we find in the experiences of men and women recounted here the promises and the warnings on which you and I must choose today to act—or to ignore.

This is the adventure of studying the Bible for adults. To study, to examine, and to hear God speak. To us as individuals.

GOING DEEPER

This chapter has provided an introduction to the time of the judges. These *Going Deeper* assignments will help you mature in your study of the book itself, to discover, on your own, personal messages from God to you. Select one of the three studies outlined below.

1. Do an in-depth study of Judges 1:1—3:6. First, read through these verses quickly, jotting down questions that may occur. For instance, you may wonder: "Chariots of iron. Did Israel ever defeat chariots? Was this really the reason for their inability to defeat the plains dwellers?" Or you may ask, "What was God's purpose in leaving the enemy nations in the land? Was it just for the purpose of punishment?"

Second, reread the passage carefully, looking for answers to your queries. (For a question like that on chariots, check a concordance. You'll find that Israel did win against chariots under Barak and Deborah. What happened then? What explains that victory?)

Third, see if you can summarize any principles from what you have discovered. (For instance, you might have asked about the relationship between the factors accounting for Israel's decline pp. 43, 44). If so, your answer might link them in a cause-effect relationship, or in a sequential way. (See if you can state a principle that expresses any relationship you see.)

Finally, write down a personal application. Record what you believe God is saying to you through what you have found in His Word.

You may find it helpful to use a form like the one on the following page (Figure V) for this study.

2. There is a principle of Biblical interpretation we can call "selection and emphasis." Events God

51

FIGURE V

WORKSHEET ON JUDGES

QUESTIONS	OBSERVATIONS	PRINCIPLES	MESSAGE TO ME

FIGURE VI
THE CYCLES

ANALYSIS OF JUDGES

	1	2	3	4	5	6	7
SIN	Did evil... Forgot Jehovah... Served Baalim					Again did evil... Many Gods	
SERVITUDE			Sold Israel to Jabin for 20 years				
SUPPLICATION		Cried to Jehovah					
SALVATION		Raised up Ehud		Rest 40 years			No deliverance!
SILENCE	3:7—11	3:12—31	4:1—5:31	6:1—8:32	8:33—9:57	10:6—12:7	13:2—16:31

selects to record in Scripture are there for a reason. We need to search for the reason these specific events rather than others were selected. Some included events are given emphasis. Thus the story of Othniel is told in four verses while the story of Jephthah takes 59 verses. Clearly Jephthah is emphasized.

Look at the listing of the judges given on p. 47, and select one emphasized judge to study. Your goal: write a three-page paper expressing how the divine emphasis on this judge is important (has application) to you.

3. Much can be learned from a careful analysis of patterns that are found in some passages of Scripture. Figure VI (preceding page) is an overall chart of the chronological section of judges. Some of the segments of the chart have been filled in. Study the Bible references and complete the chart. Then write a three-page paper explaining at least five important messages God gives us in this book. And tell how one of these messages is directed to you.

THE WAY TO DEATH

"IT'S ALL RIGHT FOR YOU if that's what you like," Danny told me. He was lying on his back in a hospital bed, his face still white from loss of blood, his forehead still pinched together with pain.

We'd been talking about my conversion, and how a relationship with Jesus made a difference in my life. The day before our conversation, Danny had tried to commit suicide. He'd taken a deer rifle and fired at his heart—and missed. Instead, he blew a hole through his side, a sofa, and a roof. Now the influence of the thirteen downers he'd swallowed just before the attempt had worn off. But not the pain.

We talked and shared—about his life and mine—for several hours. We talked freely about God's desire to bring him the peace and fulfillment that only Christ can provide. It was then that Danny, with honest approval, gave me his bless-

ing: "It's all right for you, if that's what you like."
Subjectivism.

Danny expressed the conviction of many today.
All is relative; reality is subjective. The person who
likes a religious life-style enjoys something that
has meaning "for him." The person with a drug-
culture life-style, like Danny, should be ap-
preciated too. Both ways of life—and the many
others open in our culture today—are perfectly
fine for the person who chooses them. One is not
objectively "better" than another; to insist that it is
would be to intrude on a person's freedom of
choice.

To an extent, some court decisions in the United
States have reflected just this line of thought. Recently state legislatures have been puzzling over
the question of whether homosexuals ought to be
permitted to "marry" one another. The Gay Lib-
eration movement aggressively demands the right
to be different—and to have their difference accepted as a variant, but valid, morality. Some
church bodies seem to be moving toward confirm-
ing ordination of admitted homosexuals as minis-
ters.

In one Western state, the madam of a well-
known house of prostitution ran for the
legislature—and was almost elected. Students in a
Midwest seminary went to the board to demand
the same housing privileges for male and female
students who live together as for those who are
married. The "discrimination" outraged the students' moral sensitivities, an outrage foretold by a

young woman who told me some five years ago that "immorality" had to do with exploitation of the poor—and not with one's freedom to express himself or herself sexually. She was a seminarian too.

Not long ago a United States congressman confessed to being an alcoholic (a fact long known by Washington politicians and newsmen). But he confessed only after successfully completing his reelection campaign, a campaign during which he lied again and again about the problem he later confessed.

Danny had responded to my talk about Jesus with honest appreciation and approval. But it had not touched him. In his world, distinctions between right and wrong, true and false, illusion and reality, had long been blurred. This was not the fault of drugs. It was simply another expression of a well-developed trend toward relativism and subjectivism in our society. With the moral moorings slipped, each man is free to take that "way which seemeth right unto a man," but whose end is "the ways of death" (Prov. 14:12).

A BIBLICAL ABSOLUTE

Against subjectivism and relativism, the Bible presents a bold absolute. It affirms that there are universal moral principles on which the behavior of individuals and societies must be based. If this moral base is abandoned, the individual or the society will be destroyed.

Scripture's unyielding absolute is rooted in the presupposition that ours is a moral universe. God, who shaped and planned it all, is a moral being. Creation's design expresses His moral character. This is true especially of the nature of man, which the Bible insists bears the stamp of the eternal: the "image" of God planted in us at creation. As a train is designed to run on tracks, the human personality is designed to function healthily only when stabilized by a steadfast morality. Individuals and societies which jump their moral tracks become increasingly bogged down—and ultimately are unable to function.

It would be wrong to think that morality is a stabilizing factor only for the believer. Righteousness is something that "works" for the believer and unbeliever alike. The Book of Proverbs puts it this way: "Righteousness exalteth a nation: but sin is a reproach to any people" (14: 34). There are many such observations in Proverbs. "The crookedness of the treacherous destroys them" (11: 3, RSV). "The wicked shall fall by his own wickedness" (11: 5). "The violence of the wicked will sweep them away, because they refuse to do what is just" (21: 7, RSV). In a moral universe, there are certain fixed moral laws which when violated bring destruction as a natural consequence. History is full of illustrations of this fact.

It is not that God *intervenes* to punish. It is simply that, given the nature of our universe, the abandonment of righteousness inevitably leads to dissolution of the personality or of the society.

This, of course, is part of the tragedy of Danny. He had chosen a way that seemed right to him. Even his brush with a 30-30 could not convince him that his way leads to death. Danny denied the Bible's revelation of reality and treated God's way as only one of many alternate and equally acceptable ways. This, too, is the tragedy of society after society and culture after culture. When a people chooses a way that seems right to them, but a way which ignores the divine revelation of righteousness, that society is moving toward its downfall.

The Bible is not just for believers. The Bible reveals a reality with which every man must live. He can choose to accept reality and live in harmony with it. Or he can choose to reject reality and experience its crushing weight. In either case, each demonstrates that God's Word is true. And each society will bear witness.

The men of Joshua's day demonstrated the faithfulness of God's promise; their obedience brought victory and rest. In the days of the judges, men turned away from righteousness to choose their own way. The fate of these men and the society which they developed now bear witness to the fact that rejection of the divinely ordained life-style brings despair, dissolution, and defeat.

DEMONSTRATION OF THE THEME
Judges 17–21

The middle chapters of the Book of Joshua report external disasters that came upon Israel.

Physical enemies, outside peoples, were sent by God to judge His people and bring them to repentance. These judgments were "extraordinary." That is, they were not direct natural consequences of Israel's sin but divine interventions. It does not always follow, when you and I sin or when a nation abandons righteousness that outside forces overpower us.

What does always follow is that there is inner deterioration. There is a loss of direction. There are growing conflicts. These last chapters of Judges are added to show us what happened *within* Israel as a result of abandoning God's ways. It is, in fact, the inner deterioration that is the surest evidence. Abandoning God's standards sears the conscience and confuses the ability of the individual to distinguish between good and evil. No wonder Proverbs puts it the way it does. There *is* a "way which seemeth right unto a man" (Prov. 14: 12), but that "way" is one of illusion. Yet there is also a hard reality; the reality toward which man's seeming "right" leads to death.

Lost legacy (Jdg. 17, 18). The first of three stories steps outside of the earlier chronological sequence and into the intimate context of an Israelite family. Using the cameo or slice-of-life approach, the author now moves on to demonstrate the impact of Israel's national apostasy on the life-style of individuals.

The first few verses of chapter 17 are enough to jolt us. If we're familiar with the life-style God defines for His people in the Mosaic Law, we're hardly prepared for what we see in this typical Ephraimite family. Verses 2 and 3 introduce Micah, a man who stole eleven hundred pieces of silver from his mother and, moved by fear after overhearing his mother's curse, confessed it. The curse was canceled by the mother's utterance of a blessing, and Micah restored the silver, which was then dedicated to God but used to make idols for the household shrine!

Theft within the family? Superstition and fear? Worship of idols? Shrines in the house, and abandonment of the central sanctuary? Every one of these stands in stark contrast to the righteous way ordained by God for Israel. Every one of these is characteristic of the pagan culture Israel was to drive out and to supplant.

As we read on in the story, we see additional evidence that Israel had lost its moral bearings. Initial disobedience had led to an increasing loss of moral judgment. The ways of God are increasingly confused with and supplanted by the customs of the nearby pagans.

The story of Micah goes on. Micah ordained one of his own sons to be a priest—again contrary to the Law. But when a wandering Levite (not of Aaron's priestly line) passed by, Micah hired him to "be unto me a father and a priest" (17:10). Although Micah again violated instructions given in the Law, he was thrilled at the turn of events. "Now know I that the Lord will do me good, seeing I have a Levite to my priest" (17:13).

Some time later a group of Danites (one of the

61

12 tribes) was exploring for more land to occupy. They recognized the young Levite, asked his blessing, and shortly afterward located a city in a hidden valley that was occupied by a colony of Sidonians (inhabitants of the pagan city of Sidon, near Tyre). Reporting on the successful reconnaissance, the Danites recommended the Levite to their tribe. Some 600 men stopped by on the way to the Sidonian colony and offered the young Levite a "promotion." The Bible tells us that "the priest's heart was glad" (18: 20) at this invitation. He stole the idols and other objects in Micah's shrine and gladly left his employer behind.

Micah pursued, complaining bitterly about the theft of his gods and his priest. The Danites threatened him; the betrayed man slunk sadly back home. As for the Danites, they went on to the colony town, Laish, killed all the Sidonians, and settled there. Through the period of the judges the Levite's descendants served as their priests, ministering at a worship center featuring Micah's idol.

This story is told without comment or evaluation. None is required. Over and over again the pattern of life described stands in stark contrast to the pattern prescribed in the divine revelation. Godly ways are a legacy Israel seems to have lost.

Moral decay (Jdg. 19). The second story in this section of Judges does what no commentary could. We are shown vividly the moral and interpersonal implications of the loss of the divine legacy. In this story another Levite is featured.

We're told of his marriage to a secondary wife (concubine), who angrily returned to her father's home after a spat. After four months, the Levite went to be reconciled to her—something welcomed by the father, as such a separation was both a reflection on his house and a threat to any bride price he may have received. After typical Eastern hospitality—of some five days!—the Levite and his party left to return home. As it was probably about three in the afternoon, they were unable to travel far. The Levite was unwilling to stop at Jebus (Jerusalem) because it was still occupied by pagans. Instead he went on to Gibeah, which was inhabited by Benjamites (one of the 12 tribes).

But the man was offered no hospitality, except by a temporary resident from Ephraim. (This was a violation of a basic Eastern custom.) That night the inhabitants of the city pounded on the door, announcing their intention of making the Levite a victim of homosexual assault! The Benjamites seemed on the verge of breaking in, so the Levite grabbed his concubine and thrust her outside to the men. The Scripture reports, "And they knew her [a Biblical euphemism for sexual intercourse], and abused her all the night until the morning" (19:25). In the morning when the Levite opened the door, he found the girl crumpled outside, her hands stretched out to grip the threshold—dead.

The ways that had seemed "right" to Israel led to the depths of depravity, to unbelievable moral decay and death. For far more than physical death is pictured in this incident.

■ There is the death of love. The Old Testament Law taught a person to love God and to love others as himself. Here was a Levite—who represented instruction in God's Law—selfishly thrusting his concubine out to a group of depraved madmen. The capacity to care for others dies when one deserts the ways of God.

■ There is the death of identity. The Levite and the old man with whom he stayed both showed that they viewed women as something less than human. In the Creation, woman was taken from man's ribs as a vivid affirmation of her identity with man. Woman was created second, but is not secondary. She is of the same stuff as man; with man she bears the image of God and bears the privilege of dominion (Gen. 1, 2).

With the loss of the divine viewpoint, which came with abandonment of Israel's legacy of Law, there came the loss of woman's identity. Distortion of the divine plan brought a measure of death to men and women alike, for in denying woman full humanity, man denies himself.

■ There is the death of image. Man was made in the image of God, with a personality to reflect the personality of the Creator. Even today, men choose to seek their identity in a supposed descent from the beasts—and choose to be ruled by their passions. Thus, the psalmists compare such men to brutes; Jude, too, sees them doing "by instinct like unreasoning animals" the very things which destroy them (Jude 10, NIV). The depravity exhibited by the Benjamites clearly shows the degradation which comes when men lose sight of the divine image and deny their origins in Him.

The story of Micah and the Danites set the stage for this tale of the Levite and his concubine. When men lose righteousness' way, depravity follows as night follows the waning of the day.

Conflict within (Jdg. 20, 21). These two chapters continue the story of the Levite and his concubine. Taking the body home, the Levite cut it into pieces and sent the pieces throughout Israel. Shocked, the people gathered to hear the Levite's report (which carefully avoided mentioning his own cowardly part). Shocked as much by the graphic way in which the Levite dramatized the event as by the act, the tribes angrily agreed to punish Gibeah.

When the men of Benjamin would not surrender their relatives in Gibeah, a civil war resulted. Many thousands were killed, and the tribe of Benjamin was all but wiped out.

How different from the incident reported in Joshua 22, where all of Israel was ready to war to keep some from beginning to sin! No discipline had been exercised to restrain sin from developing (the Law had commanded homosexuals to be put to death). The war came when part of Israel proved unwilling to surrender murderers to justice!

Morality is never just an individual or personal thing. The strands which hold society together, which provide security for its members, are rooted in morality. When righteousness is abandoned and ways that "seem right" to men are allowed to substitute for the divine standards, the society itself has begun to rush down the road toward its own death.

ON THE ROCK

Scripture does not argue or explain the universal truths which are God's firm expression of reality. Rather, the Bible tends to affirm—and to demonstrate. God's Word is true, not only because God is a trustworthy person and it is He who has spoken, but because the Word which God speaks is in complete harmony with reality. That human experience conforms to the principles expressed in Scripture does not "prove" the Bible, but human experience does serve to demonstrate its reliability and its relevance.

This is the function of this section of Judges as well, and the function of many of the Old Testament stories. They demonstrate and illustrate the reliability of the affirmations of God's Word. Through Moses and through Joshua, God had told Israel plainly that commitment to Him and to His ways would bring them blessing. "Righteousness exalts a nation" was true then and is true now. The reliability of that principle is seen in the experience of Joshua's own generation and the rest which they won.

But the same Word of God through Moses and Joshua had warned that disobedience carries within it the seeds of its own destruction. The time of Judges graphically demonstrates this truth.

The process of deterioration may take a longer or a shorter time. The bitter and deadly fruit may require several generations to mature. But the Word of God is reliable. The death it foretells will come. Unshakable and unbreakable, the Word expresses the realities by which men live, whether they choose to live for God or not.

GOING DEEPER
to personalize

1. Read Judges 17—21, underlining everything you see that is out of harmony with the life-style prescribed for Israel by the Law.

2. Psalm 12 seems to fit the period described in Judges (as well as other times in Israel's history) quite well. What insights does it give?

3. Imagine that someone in our society were writing Psalm 12 today. List all the things about which you feel he might be writing.

4. One phrase that keeps reappearing in these chapters of Judges is: "In those days there was no king in Israel: every man did that which was right in his own eyes" (21:25). Today the courts tend to define obscenity by the standards of the community. What do you think of this rule as a valid measure? Is there any relationship between this phrase from Judges and the modern judicial trend? What?

5. If someone were to describe our society today, where would they place it on a continuum ranging from the righteousness that marked Israel in

Joshua's day to the unrighteousness marking Israel as described in 17—21? Make your own check mark on this continuum below, and be prepared to justify your positioning.

[righteous———————————————unrighteous]

to probe

Gibbon's *Decline and Fall of the Roman Empire* describes Rome's breakdown in five factors. Find out what these are, and see what their relationship might be to the situation described here in Judges.

Then check. Have similar factors been associated with declines in other societies and cultures?

SOCIETY, OR ME?

THE TEENAGER STANDS before the juvenile court judge. Who's to blame? The home? The society? The individual? These questions reflect one of the most significant disputes of our day: the struggle between the notion that society shapes and determines the individual—and the notion that the individual bears full responsibility for his acts. Pleas to juries, much of our social legislation, various schools in psychology and sociology, and the supposed philosophies of our political parties all reflect the conflict between these two ideas.

How much of a person's choice is determined by social conditions and how much by the individual's free volition is a tangled question. There's no doubt that both environment and society do shape personality. This is one reason why Israel's lifestyle under the Law placed so much emphasis on discipline. The people of Israel were to judge and

69

cleanse themselves from the sinful patterns which would emerge in the community. The people were jointly responsible to maintain their society. When righteousness marked the life-style of the nation, promised blessings included the eradication of social ills.

Israel, under Joshua, did maintain a just society. But there was no guarantee that individuals would continue to choose God's ways. The nation did drift away—from trust in God and from commitment to His righteous ways. Israel increasingly became an unjust society, with all the sin and insensitivity we see portrayed in Judges 17—21. The society as a whole became ungodly.

What about the individual then? Did an unjust society, amplifying the tendency to evil which sin has implanted in the human personality, make it impossible for the individual to choose good? The last chapters of Judges gave us insight into the deterioration of Israel as a whole through the description of two people whose experiences reflect the whole nation.

Now we turn to three cameo portraits of individuals who give us insight into the private lives of men and women in that same paganized culture. These individuals—one private and two public personages—reveal something of the complex interplay between the shaping power of the environment and the freedom of the individual to choose. In examining their lives, we may also see something of the challenge facing us. For you and I live in an unjust and unrighteous society as well, one which reflects values and a morality which are far from the divine ideal. Our view of our world and ourselves may help us understand choices we face which were also faced by the men and women who lived in the evil days when "there was no King in Israel."

THREE WHO CHOSE

The Bible gives a surprising amount of space to the days of the judges. Israel passed some 400 years in Egypt, and about these years the Bible is silent. Yet, chapter after chapter portrays in depth the life God's people lived during the 300 or so years of Israel's deterioration. It follows that God recorded these stories of men and women, as well as the tale of the nation, for a purpose. Through the inspired record God communicates His message—to the generations of Israelites who lived later, and to us who live today.

Ruth (Ruth 1–4). When Elimelech took his wife, Naomi, and two sons to the land of Moab, one of Israel's traditional enemies, he was fleeing a famine. He was also leaving his heritage in Israel. During the following ten years, Elimelech died and Naomi's two sons married Moabite wives. Within that decade, the two boys also died, and Naomi, hearing that the days of famine were over in Israel, determined to return.

At first the two daughters-in-law intended to return to Israel with her. But Naomi urged them to stay in Moab. There seemed no hope of mar-

71

riage or a home for them if they returned with the now bitter widow. One listened to Naomi's urging and returned to her people and her gods. The other, Ruth, made one of the most touching and courageous statements of individual commitment recorded in Scripture. Abandoning her people and culture, Ruth chose to identify herself with Naomi, Naomi's people, and Naomi's God (1:16, 17).

The Book of Ruth traces the return of the two women and the outcome of Ruth's commitment. We see her commitment was worked out in her personal life-style. Even though a foreigner, she was recognized as one who had come to take refuge under the wings of the Lord God of Israel (2:8-13).

The story of Ruth continues with her meeting Boaz, a relative of her dead husband. In Old Testament times, it was customary for a widow who did not return to her father's household to marry someone in her husband's family. The nearest kinsman had this privilege and obligation. The first child of such a second marriage was given the inheritance of the first husband, rather than inheriting from his actual father's holdings, particularly if the second husband had been previously married and had a family of his own.

With Ruth's reputation and her faith in God established, Boaz was drawn to this young widow. He agreed to marry her and take responsibility for Elimelech's inheritance. With many fascinating insights into the customs of those days, Boaz cleared away the legal requirements and married Ruth.[1]

The last verses of the Book of Ruth contain a striking revelation: the child born to Ruth and Boaz (and "given" to Naomi as a grandson) was Obed, the grandfather of Israel's greatest and most God-fearing king, David.

Samson (Jdg. 13–16). Four Old Testament chapters are allotted to Ruth; four are also given to Samson. Very possibly, Samson was a contemporary of Obed or of Ruth herself.

Ruth had been born in a pagan home, and later, influenced by Naomi, had chosen to identify herself with Israel and Israel's God—even though at the time Israel was an oppressed people. Samson was born in Israel, and his birth was preannounced by an angel. His father and mother were a godly and believing pair. The response they made to the angel clearly demonstrates that. When his wife told him an angel had spoken to her, Manoah prayed and asked that the angel be sent again to instruct them in how to bring up the child. When the angel came, Manoah's first words demonstrate a show of strong faith: "Now when your words come true, what is to be the boy's manner of life, and what is he to do?" (13:12, RSV).

The pair were taught that the boy was to be dedicated to God from his birth, never to drink wine or cut his hair or eat any unclean thing. This pattern of life is defined in the Old Testament for

[1] In reading Ruth 3:16-18, it's important to note that this action had symbolic significance, expressing Ruth's willingness to place herself under the protection of Boaz. There is no immorality involved in this incident.

those taking a special vow to God. Such persons were called Nazirites. From his birth, Samson knew an ideal environment. The Bible tells us that "the boy grew, and the Lord blessed him. And the Spirit of the Lord began to stir him" (13:24, 25, RSV).

This promising start soon drifted into a disturbing pattern of life. Samson, for all his advantages, was a selfish and sensual man. He was not motivated by a concern for God's people; in fact, the Lord had to use his passion for a Philistine woman to move Samson against His people's enemies (see 14:1-4). Engaged to the girl he had desired, Samson was tricked into the loss of a bet with guests at a wedding feast. Angry because the girl had betrayed the answer to the riddle over which he had bet, Samson paid—then disappeared in hot anger (14:9). His bride was given to another man!

Furious, Samson took revenge by burning the Philistines' fields and beginning a one-man guerrilla warfare against Israel's oppressors. Instead of leading his people to throw off Philistine dominion, Samson continued to act alone, being moved only by his own thirst for revenge. Ultimately Samson's own people were forced to guarantee to deliver him to their enemies or face destruction! Samson went with them, but when the Israelites had left, Samson broke off the bonds that held him and, grabbing a donkey's jawbone, used it as a weapon to kill a thousand enemies (15:10-20).

Samson was clearly invulnerable. He possessed a supernatural physical strength, so unnatural that the lords of the Philistines realized there must be some secret to it—and some way to neutralize it. Samson's strength became his weakness; his dominance over others was based on physical vitality. His weakness was the dominance of the desires of his flesh over him. Samson became involved with a prostitute named Delilah, who was bribed by the Philistines to seek the source of his power. Judges 16 tells how Samson foolishly betrayed his secret—his long hair, which had never been cut and which symbolized his Nazirite commitment. Once his hair was cut, he was easily taken by the Philistines, blinded and forced to grind grain at a mill in a Gaza prison.

Much later, the Philistines gathered to praise their god Dagon for giving Samson, "the ravager of our country" (16:24, RSV), into their power. Samson was brought in to be ridiculed. Leaning against the two middle pillars which bore the weight of the great temple, Samson, his hair now regrown, prayed for strength. With a mighty heave, he displaced the pillars, and the temple crumpled, killing him and some 3,000 of the enemy.

Samson had judged Israel for 20 years. Yet he is the only one of all the judges of whom it is not recorded that he brought rest to the land.

Samuel (I Sam. 1:1–8:10). Samuel is often considered the last of the judges and the first of the prophets—the transition figure between this extended period of Israel's history and the establishment of a monarchy.

75

Samuel was born in answer to the prayer of his mother, Hannah, and was dedicated to the Lord before his birth (I Sam. 1). At age three, he was "loaned to the Lord" (see 1:28); his parents brought him to the Tabernacle at Shiloh to serve God under the guidance of Eli, the priest.

The Bible makes it clear that while Eli himself was a godly man, his two sons were not. These priests used their position to take the best of the sacrificed meat for themselves (in direct disobedience to God's Law); their servants used force against those who had come to worship; and they used their position to seduce the women who served at the Tabernacle (2:12-21). While Eli rebuked them, he did not discipline or restrain them as he should have done (2:22-25). Finally, God pronounced the judgment that Eli should have determined long before (2:27-36).

Samuel, however, growing up in the Tabernacle under Eli's tutelage, took a very different road. While Samuel was still a child, God spoke to him, and he responded. Soon all Israel realized that this lad was selected to be a prophet.

In due course, the judgment announced by God against Eli's family came. The two sons fell in battle; Eli collapsed and died; and the Ark of the Covenant was taken by the Philistines. In a miraculous way, reported in I Samuel 5 and 6, the Ark was restored. Samuel led a revival in which Israel put away the gods of the foreigners. God in response "thundered ... against" (7:10) the Philistines when they brought up an army to attack the revived Israel. The Philistines were routed and had to withdraw from Israel's territory. Samuel, who then functioned simultaneously as a prophet and priest and judge, "judged Israel all the days of his life" (7:15) and administered justice to a people who again knew rest from oppression.

But again the choice of godliness did not automatically cross to the next generation! First Samuel 8:1 tells us that when he was old, Samuel made his sons judges. And the Scripture records that "his sons did not walk in his ways, but turned aside after gain; they took bribes and perverted justice" (I Sam. 8:3, RSV).

THE THIRD FACTOR
Deut. 11:18-21

The three portraits of godly men and women of the times of the judges focus our attention on an even more important issue. In each of these settings, we find striking sketches of families.

Ruth, brought up in a pagan setting, turned from her upbringing to identify with a holy people and their God. Samson, child of a godly home, dedicated to God, lived for himself. Even in his death, Samson's primary motive was a selfish one: "Strengthen me . . . O God, that I may be avenged upon the Philistines for one of my two eyes" (Jdg. 16:28, RSV).

Eli was a godly man. Yet his two sons chose the pursuit of evil. Samuel, brought up in the same environment, responded to God and not only

77

lived an exemplary personal life but also led Israel in a great spiritual revival. Yet Samuel's own sons did not follow Samuel's ways!

What can we conclude from this record? First, environment alone does not determine us for either good or evil. There is an element of freedom and of responsibility that must be accepted by each of us. We cannot blame our parents, our friends, or our society for the choices we make. A bad environment may make it more difficult to choose the right. But the individual still remains responsible for his acts. In the same way, a godly environment is no guarantee that one will choose wisely. We can take no comfort in our parents' faith; we need to make our own personal commitment lest we, too, wander from God's way.

Second, there seems to be an interplay in the Book of Judges between three factors—not just two. Rather than seeing the key factor as the influence of society against the individual's freedom to choose, a complex interplay is suggested between the society, the individual, and the home. Judges shows that even in a corrupt society there were godly men and women and godly families. It also shows compellingly the need for believers to understand how to share faith with their children so as to encourage a personal choice of commitment to and trust in God.

How can parents provide a godly environment which encourages their children to choose God? The Old Testament, reinforced by the New, gives these principles:

Parental response is a prerequisite (Deut. 11:18). The command is to "lay up these words of mine in your heart and in your soul" (RSV). This does not mean that the parent must be perfect, an "ideal" believer who never makes a mistake or fails. Instead, it means that the parent's faith must be more than a Sunday observance, more than giving lip service to God and His Word. Knowing a great deal about the Bible is not stressed here. What is important is that the parent be a person *who responds* to God's Word, building its messages into his/her heart and soul. God's revelation is to shape attitudes and values and behaviors as well as beliefs.

Only a person growing in the Lord can communicate His reality compellingly to others.

Personal relationship is the context (Deut. 11:19). The Scriptures focus the privilege of communicating God and His ways to each new generation in the home: "You shall teach them to your children" (RSV). Israel's life-style did include certain institutions, such as the cities of refuge and the Levitical cities. But there were no educational institutions. There was no Sunday school for the nurture of the new generations or colleges for their instruction to the faith![2] The home, with its intimate "you . . . your" relationship, was the context in which faith was to be—and is to be!—communicated.

The rest of Scripture shows us why this is so

[2] By Jesus' time there was organized instruction of children in each community. The children learned to read and write, and their text was the Scripture. But this was not comparable to present church educational institutions.

important. Faith is best communicated when there is a love relationship between the teacher and learner. Where there is opportunity to observe the life and participate in shared experiences, the values, attitudes, and emotions that accompany actions are learned as well as beliefs. Where there is a chance for the communicator to explain in words his inner feelings and thoughts, God's standards can be viewed incarnated. Where the relationship is a continuing one, extending over the growing years, and not simply infrequent contact with a variety of different "teachers," the life-style can be gradually developed.

Critical relational principles shown in Scripture seem to be these: loving, continuing, being close, openly communicating, sharing. There is no better place for such relationships to be developed and to grow than in the intimacy of the family.

Explicit teaching is to infuse daily life (Deut. 11:19). The passage says that we are to teach God's words to our children by talking to them "when you are sitting in your house, and when you are walking by the way, and when you lie down, and when you rise" (RSV). The stress here is not on formal teaching or organized classes, but on explaining the meaning of God's Word as experiences are shared between parent and child.

Yesterday morning a conflict flared up between my youngest son and my daughter. He said something thoughtless that hurt her feelings. After I spent ten minutes of quieting and helping her, my son was angry at me. He felt she had taken his

80

remark wrongly, and so it was her fault. I'd been altogether too comforting to suit him!

It took about a half hour to work things through with him, and help him see that his words had been thoughtless, that he really had spoken in anger, selfishly. It took even more time to come to the place where forgiveness could be asked and given. Then we talked more about forgiveness, that for the Christian it means the confessed sin is forgiven and washed out, gone, forgotten. "I will forgive their wickedness, and will remember their sins no more" (Heb. 8:12, NIV) is God's promise.

Later that day, our youngest was going over to play with a friend with whom he'd had some conflict. My wife remarked on that conflict. Didn't it bother him to go over again? "No," he answered. "When you've forgiven someone, you forget."

It is this kind of teaching of God's ways, using His Word to interpret and guide in daily experiences, that is the key to Christian nurture. It was this kind of teaching which could have helped Israel to avoid their experiences during the days of the judges. It is this kind of teaching which can help the new generation of today discover God's reality and make personal choices to trust God and to commit themselves to Him.

GOING DEEPER
to personalize

1. Read carefully at least two of the following passages which describes life during the time of

the judges: Ruth; Judges 13—16; I Samuel 1:1—8:10.

2. Select one of the three people focused on in the text and write a short page biographical sketch. Include the following items: His or her character as an adult, factors which influenced his character development, personal decisions that were pivotal and the motivation for those decisions, his or her strengths and weaknesses, what we can learn from this person's life.

3. Looking at the three keys for effective family life (pp. 79, 80), (a) evaluate your own childhood home in terms of each factor; (b) if you have children of your own, evaluate your own family lifestyle now.

4. Which of the following things do you feel has played the largest part in your own development to date: (a) society? (b) your home? (c) your own personal choices? How have each of these factors affected you?

to probe

1. To see the description of Old Testament and New Testament education of children, read William Barclay, *Educational Ideals in the Ancient World* (Baker).

2. Write to the author, Larry Richards, % Renewal Research Associates, 14411 No. 6th St., Phoenix, AZ 85022, for a free brochure on family education.

6

I Samuel 7–31

IN SEARCH OF UTOPIA

FOR MANY THOUSANDS OF YEARS, men have
dreamed of utopia. Plato, the Greek philosopher,
wrote the *Republic* to explain his ideas about the
ideal state. Rousseau, a French philosopher, and
many, many others have explored the notion that
if only a perfect social system existed, all social and
personal evils would be eradicated. Human life
would be joyful, selfishness rooted out, poverty
and injustice would disappear.

Utopian thinking persists today. Many young
people have a utopian view of marriage. Once the
vows are said, and the lovers united, they believe
all will be "happy forever after." Utopian thinking
often invades the church; we are dissatisfied with
our local bodies because they haven't yet recov-
ered the total New Testament experience. Many
today desire communal living; often the idea is
that in a setting of closeness, deep and satisfying
fellowship will quickly come.

83

But man's utopian dreams have never been fulfilled. The perfect state, the Camelot community, wavers like the mirage it is when we reach out to touch it. In fact, the life-style given Israel by God in the Mosaic Law is the only possible prescription for utopia which the world has ever known. For a time, during the days of Joshua's generation, utopia seemed within Israel's grasp. But then the people turned from God and, in turning from Him, lost all chance for a whole and healthy society.

The message is clear. No social system (not even the best!) can function unless the individuals within it are committed to love and to obey God.

THE MESSAGE MISUNDERSTOOD
I Samuel 7–8

The history of the judges demonstrates over and over again that the critical element in any society is the relationship of its members to God. When Israel sinned, oppressors came; when Israel turned to God, they were given restoration and rest. Samuel, the last of the judges, led a spiritual revival, and God enabled Israel to push back the Philistines who occupied major sections of Israel's Promised Land. This was a truly striking victory. The Philistines had iron weapons, for they knew the secrets of working that metal. The Israelites, as an oppressed people, had few weapons and no iron. In a later battle, only King Saul and his son Jonathan had swords; the men of Israel had to use

84

farm implements as weapons (I Sam. 13:19-22). Yet victory came—through God's enablement and intervention. During the time of the judges Israel was a theocracy; God Himself was their King. When the men of Israel committed themselves to follow Him, He fought their battles for them.

We have seen how, when Samuel grew old, he made his sons judges. They fell short of the standard Samuel set, and the people of Israel yearned for a king. "We will have a king over us," they demanded, "then we shall be like other nations, with a king to govern us, to lead us out to war and fight our battles" (I Sam. 8:19, 20, NEB).

There was nothing wrong in itself with the idea of a monarchy. The Old Testament earlier had foretold a day when Israel would have a king. But now Israel's motives were terribly wrong and their awareness of the issues was as shallow and vague as is the awareness of modern utopians. Under the Mosaic constitution, God had called them to be different from all the nations. God had promised that He Himself would rule over them and govern them. God Himself promised to go out before them and fight their battles. Now, in a very definite and explicit way, Israel overtly rejected God and the theocracy.

Samuel warned Israel about the ways of human government (I Sam. 8:10-18). More and more of the people's resources would be demanded to support the governmental structure and a growing bureaucracy. The burden of taxes would rise. Their children would be pressed into government

85

service and the army. The day would come when they would cry out to God about their king and his oppressions, and God would not respond. The choice Israel was making was an irrevocable one.

Still the people insisted. They had not understood from their history the message God had repeated over and over again: "It is relationship with Me that brings you health and wholeness." Looking away from God, Israel looked for a better system of government as the answer to their problems and needs.

Samuel was deeply hurt by this demand, feeling it was a rejection of him and his leadership. He turned to God in prayer and was told to listen to the voice of the people. Their rejection was not of Samuel, but of God (8: 6-9). Israel was responding as they always had since the days of their deliverance from Egypt. In poignant words, God told Samuel, "Ever since I brought them from Egypt they have continually forsaken me and followed other gods" (I Sam. 8: 8, TLB).

God knew what it was for His people to reject Him. He knows it today—and suffers just as you or I would. Yet His love remains firm. He continues to care for us and to teach us.

SAUL, ISRAEL'S FIRST KING
I Samuel 9–31

We have to see Saul as a man through whom God continues to teach Israel. Like every human being,

Saul made his own choices and shaped his own destiny. Yet, in God's selection of Saul as Israel's first king, we can also see that God was instructing His people. Saul, the man with great potential but with a tragic flaw, demonstrated dramatically that Israel under the morarchy still had to depend upon commitment to the Lord.

Saul's early leadership (I Sam. 9–12). The early portrait of Saul is attractive. We see him as modest (10: 17-25) and wise (11: 11-15). We also see Saul as a strong military leader, willing to give the Lord credit rather than claim it for himself (11: 13). His vigorous leadership and bravery gave heart to the Hebrew people. The Bible says, "He did valiantly . . . and delivered Israel out of the hands of those who plundered them" (14: 48, RSV). His potential and his early performance were great.

Tests of leadership (I Sam. 13, 15). But Saul was overridden by weaknesses in his character.

His first test is recorded in I Samuel 13. Gathering a small army to battle an invading host of Philistines, Saul was told to wait for Samuel to come and offer sacrifice. Samuel was to come within seven days. Yet, as each day passed, more of Saul's army slipped away. Seeing the people scattering, Saul finally would wait no longer. Later, telling an angry Samuel of his fears, Saul said, "I felt compelled to make the whole-offering myself" (13: 12, NEB).

Centuries earlier, another newly appointed leader, Joshua, had been told to march his people in dead silence around a walled city. Without any deviation from the divine instruction, Joshua had obeyed the apparently meaningless directions. Now Saul also had been given a seven-day test. But Saul's resolve failed. He disobeyed!

The first qualification of a spiritual leader is that he must follow the instructions of God fully and completely.

A second test showed a widening of the distrust Saul had demonstrated. Sent against another enemy with instructions to totally destroy them and their wealth, Saul let his people take spoil, and he even kept the enemy king alive (15: 3, 14-16). Saul gave another excuse that showed his inner weakness: "I have disobeyed your instructions and the command of the Lord, for I was afraid of the people and did what they demanded" (15: 24, TLB). Without courage to lead Israel to obey God, Saul began to fear man's opinion. By failing to trust and obey God, he had lost that inner moral authority on which all leadership ultimately rests. Then he followed, not led, his people.

The downward path (I Sam. 16–31). The rest of I Samuel traces Saul's deterioration as a leader and as a person. The once brave leader, aware that he had been rejected by the God he abandoned (16: 14), quaked with fear when faced with Goliath's challenge (I Sam. 17). When David, the young shepherd, killed the giant warrior, and was later praised by the people for surpassing Saul in battle, Saul's jealousy led him to become David's enemy. Ultimately, in desperate old age, cut off from God and His guidance, Saul resorted to demonic sources for guidance, an act for which he himself had earlier decreed the death penalty (28: 9).

The next day Saul died in battle.

Handsome, valiant, decisive, and modest, Saul still failed as a leader. And Israel was shown again that the flaw which prevents experience of God's best was within *them*—not in society. Only full commitment to God and reliance on Him expressed in trusting obedience can lead individuals, families, churches, or societies to health and wholeness. This message, implicit in the total history of the time of the judges, is made tragically clear in Israel's first king. The system was new. But the issue remained the same.

Man's response to God, not the kind of social system under which he lives, is and always will be the key.

THE YEARS OF DARKNESS
A Summary

The Bible is an accurate historical record. At the same time it is a *selective* record; the events reported have been carefully chosen by God's Spirit, who inspired and directed the authors. What's more, the events have been selected to demonstrate principles which are stated explicitly in the direct teaching of the Scriptures.

The goal of Bible study for the believer is not only to master content but to become sensitive to the messages which God communicates through the written record. Seeing the outworking of Biblical truths in individuals and cultures, we gain fresh insights into the life-style God calls us to today.

What messages are emphasized in the passages of Scripture we've examined so far? They develop this central theme: trust in God, expressed as obedient response, is the critical issue in the believer's life. Such trust leads to blessing. Lack of trust, expressed as it will invariably be in incomplete obedience or overt rebellion, leads to disaster.

Each segment of these Scriptures adds insights into the development of this central theme. The deeper our insight into the complex interrelationships of life, the more clearly we can recognize the implications involved in the choices which each of us is called on to make.

The following chart will help you to review and define for yourself the messages in these passages of God's Word. Sample messages are listed on the chart below. Complete it by reviewing, then adding your own insights into the messages and implications for your life.

GOING DEEPER
to personalize

1. Read carefully the following key passages of I Samuel: chapters 7, 8, 12 (establishing the monarchy); chapters 13, 15, 18, 22, 28 (the flawed king).

YEARS OF DARKNESS, DAYS OF GLORY

Passage	"Messages" I See	Applied to Me
Judges 1—3	1. 2. 3.	
Judges 3—16 (overview)	1. God always keeps the door open for us to return to Him 2. 3.	
Judges 17—21	1. Individuals have a moral responsibility to society 2. 3.	
Ruth	1. 2. 3.	
I Samuel 1—8	1. 2. 3.	
I Samuel 7—31 (Saul's Life)	1. 2. 3.	

91

2. Complete at least two of the chart sections. (See PROBE 2 and 3 for guidelines.)

3. The Old Testament theme here seems to convey the idea that the form of government under which men live is *not* the key to personal or to societal health. There are four forms of government with which we are relatively familiar now. What do you see as the strengths or weaknesses of each of these four:

a) O.T. theocracy

b) monarchy

c) Western democracy (capitalism)

d) communistic state

What do you believe the Christian's attitude toward (or under) each of these should be? Why?

4. What is the most significant thing you can do now to influence:

a) your family

b) your community

c) your country

Which of these do you believe is part of the believer's responsibility, and how might that responsibility be met?

to probe

1. How would you argue in a debate for the following proposition: Resolved: It was not God's will for Israel to have a king. How would you argue against it?

2. Review the years of darkness this section of Scripture (Judges—I Samuel 8) has revealed, and complete the "messages" chart on page 91. Re-

member that this chart is designed to help you record your insights and the implication you see for yourself.

3. At the same time, you'll want to check your insights. Do others see the same or similiar principles? Can you demonstrate that the ideas you have expressed are really shown by events or express statements of Scripture? When you share your insights, do others recognize them as valid? Are these messages expressed elsewhere in Old or New Testament statements?

Often God will use the Scriptures to suggest something to individuals that is particularly meaningful and is clearly God's guidance in a particular situation. But such personal guidance shouldn't be mistaken for a universal principle applicable to everyone at all times. Yet, there *are* universal principles. For instance, on the chart section for Judges 3—16, there is the notation, "God always keeps the door open for us to return to Him." We see this principle illustrated in the seven cycles: God did not cast Israel off even after *repeated* sin. And the New Testament encourages us to come boldly to God's throne for mercy as well as grace to help (Heb. 4: 16). Thus, this message *is* one "for all people at all times."

Go over, then, the messages you listed, and determine which are personal guidance insights (mark with a P) and which are universal principles (U).

PART II
DAYS OF GLORY
David and Solomon
1010-931 B.C.

INTRODUCTION

With the death of Saul, Israel's years of frustration and failure came to an end. God gave Israel a king whom He called "a man after my own heart" (Acts 13:22, NIV). This man, David, through his deep commitment to the Lord and His many talents, led God's people to strength and freedom and power.

David's appearance marks the beginning of the days of Israel's ancient glory. During the lifetime of David and of his son Solomon, Israel saw the fulfillment of a hope which God holds out to all believers: the promise that commitment to Him will bring the showers of blessing.

THE MAKING OF A MAN

GREATNESS IS SOMETHING many people desire but few understand. Usually we recognize the great after they have achieved, after their military victories have been won, their artistic talents have gained awards, their administrative skills have brought success. What we see is the "finished product," not the process. And so we romanticize greatness.

The same thing happens in the Christian realm. The new believer who dreams of the day when he will do great things for God, the person who yearns for the time when he will be able to live a victorious and constantly exciting life, has romanticized spiritual greatness. He has missed the point that quality of life and character are developed through a process. Yearning for the product, we often rebel against the process—and in our rebellion miss the pathway that God intends to use to bring us to maturity.

It's easy to romanticize a man like David, the

shepherd boy who killed Goliath and went on to become Israel's greatest king. But the Bible doesn't let us make this kind of idealistic error. Instead, Scripture plunges us into a careful account of David and his greatness—and exposes the suffering that marked his life.

There are two rich sources for our understanding of David. The first is the historical account found in I and II Samuel, I Kings, and I Chronicles. The second source is the psalms written by David himself, psalms which express his rich emotional life and reveal his attitudes and feelings at various stages of his life. We need to explore both these sources. We need to probe them, because the man David is the key that unlocks the door of understanding to the greatest period of Israel's national existence. In David we see the qualities which brought Israel to greatness. But even more, we need to probe these sources because David stands as a model for you and me.

Like us, David was a man who often failed, who was subject to temptation and to sin. Like us, David knew despair and fear, doubt and loneliness. Like us, David had a personal relationship with God— and found in this relationship the way to live above and beyond his potential. As we explore David's life, we'll meet those qualities which can lift us to whatever greatness God calls us in our own role in life—in our home, our church, our circle of friends. And we can come to understand something more of the process through which God is now at work to make us great.

THE EARLIEST YEARS
I Samuel 16, 17; Psalms 19, 23, 29

When we first meet David, we see him in the spotlight. David had come with food to Israel's encampment where a citizen army was drawn up to fight the Philistines. But the whole army was immobilized by fear of a giant, Goliath, some nine feet tall and magnificently proportioned, who had challenged Israel to send out a man to single combat. This test of champions had been delayed; all Israel feared the giant's power.

Young David, probably still in his teens, was amazed. Certainly no pagan defying the army of the living God had a chance of victory! The Lord would deliver the man who accepted the challenge.

Saul (the king for whom Israel asked in order that he—the largest man in Israel—might fight their battles for them!) heard about David's remarks. David was sent for, and he boldly affirmed that he would fight the giant and kill him. As a shepherd, David had battled lions and bears to preserve his sheep. Surely the Lord would deliver him from the hand of the Philistine giant, for David was going in the Lord's name to battle now for His sheep!

We know the story well. David came without armor to meet the massive warrior. With a shepherd's sling, he hurled a stone which stunned Goliath. Taking the giant's massive sword, David cut off his head. Israel then pursued the demoralized Philistines into their own land.

This familiar scene is not really the beginning of David's story. The beginning is rooted in his silent years as a shepherd. It is rooted in the fear David must have felt of the wild beasts, in the courage that was tested over and over again as he went out to meet challenges with a growing trust in God.

The beginning is also found in God's Word to Samuel, who earlier had been sent to anoint this same shepherd as Israel's future king. Samuel had looked admiringly on the tallest of David's brothers. But God reminded his prophet, "The Lord sees not as man sees; man looks on the outward appearance, but the Lord looks on the heart" (16: 7, RSV).

During the lonely years of shepherding, David developed a heart for God. He learned to view God as *his* Shepherd (Ps. 23), seeing in his own ministry to his sheep God's commitment to care for His people. Living in the open, David sensed God's greatness in creation. He later wrote,

The heavens tell out the glory of God,
the vault of heaven reveals his handiwork.
Psalm 19:1 (NEB)

This same theme is often echoed in his psalms, such as Psalm 29, in which David calls men to ascribe glory to God for all that He reveals of Himself in nature.

The voice of the Lord is upon the waters:
the God of glory thundereth:

the Lord is upon many waters.
The voice of the Lord is powerful;
  the voice of the Lord is full of majesty.

Psalm 29:3, 4

The silent formative years, the weeks spent alone on the hills and valleys of Palestine tending sheep, deepened the youth's sense of God's greatness and power. David's heart responded to creation's revelation. His eyes saw the glory of the Lord.

Measured against this vision of the Lord, whose majestic voice spoke in the thunder, David saw Goliath in true perspective. The giant was merely a creature. The Lord was God.

EARLY ADVANCEMENT
I Samuel 18–22

David's stunning victory over Goliath brought its reward. He was taken into the household of Saul. There David had already established a reputation as the sweet singer of Israel, for his musical talents had soothed Saul, who was subject to demonic oppression (16: 14, 15, 23). But the people's praise of David aroused Saul's jealousy. Several times Saul tried to kill David (18: 10, 11).

David was given military command and gained a stunning series of successes (18: 12-16). Finally Saul plotted to have David killed by the Philistines; he sent David on an expedition into enemy territory, promising that his daughter Michal would

101

become David's wife if he succeeded. David carried off the "impossible" mission, and the disgruntled Saul fulfilled his part of the bargain.

First Samuel 19 and 20 tell of David's growing friendship with Jonathan, Saul's son who knew of God's intention that David would one day be king. The generous Jonathan gladly accepted God's will and allied himself with David against his father. Finally the situation so deteriorated that David was forced to flee for his life.

This was a time of strain for David. He knew extreme ups and downs, alternating between great successes with adulation from the people, and periods when he lived as a fugitive. Psalm 59 tells us of David's feelings during this time, surging from fear to anger to hope. The psalm begins:

Deliver me from my enemies, O my God,
protect me from those who rise up against me,
deliver me from those who work evil,
and save me from bloodthirsty men.

Psalm 59:1, 2

Soon David's anger was aroused by the injustice of it all:

Rouse thyself, come to my help, and see!
    Thou, Lord God of hosts, art God of Israel.
Awake to punish all the nations;
    spare none of those who treacherously plot
evil.

Psalm 59:4, 5

It seemed incomprehensible to David that God would let his enemies do such things to him. In fact, David was rather upset at the Lord for permitting it!

However, David found the strength to endure the growing pressure by reminding himself of who the Lord is, and reaffirming his trust in God:

I will sing aloud of thy steadfast love . . . .
For thou hast been to me a fortress and a
  refuge in the day of my distress.
O my Strength, I will sing praises to thee,
  for thou, O God, art my fortress,
  the God who shows me steadfast love.

Psalm 59:16, 17 (RSV)

David had been anointed king by Samuel. But David was not ready yet; he had to undergo testing. Like his descendant, Jesus, he had to learn "obedience from what he suffered" (Heb. 5:8, NIV).

God uses stress in this way in all our lives. He does not rebuke our feelings of frustration or fear or even anger. But He wants us to learn to bring our feelings and needs to Him and to let the times of testing do their character-building work.

YEARS OF PERSECUTION
I Samuel 23–31

The years that followed David's flight were agonizing ones. Saul, determined to kill David and

103

establish a dynasty, pursued him. Cities which David had helped to deliver from Israel's enemies were quick to betray their deliverer to Saul to gain the king's favor! The continual strain began to tell on the young leader; at times David knew deep despair and despondency.

The tremendous stress on David and his response to it are illustrated in the events recorded in I Samuel 26, 27. Saul received a report of David's latest hiding place and rushed there with 3,000 men. The army camped near David; that night he and Abishai, a follower, eluded the sentries and stood over their sleeping enemy. Able to kill Saul with the king's own spear, David refused. God had chosen Saul. As God's anointed, Saul could not be murdered and the killer remain guiltless. God Himself had to depose Saul in His own time. David disciplined himself to wait.

The next morning David stood on a nearby mountain crag and shouted down to Saul and his general, Abner. He showed them Saul's spear which he had taken away to demonstrate that he could have killed the sleeping king. Saul, admitting his wrong, blessed David and stopped his pursuit. *But this change of heart was temporary, and David knew it would be!*

Immediately after David's victory over what must have been a terrible temptation, David thought, "One of these days I shall be killed by Saul" (27:1, NEB). As with us, victory was followed by an emotional letdown, and despair.

In his despondency David fled to the land of

Israel's enemies, Philistia. He was given a city by a Philistine lord, and from that city he led his men on raids into distant countries. He let the Philistines believe that his forays were against Israel. Soon David was viewed as a trusted servant of Achish, lord of the city of Gath, one of the Philistines' five key city-states.

Psalm 142 tells something of David's feelings during the time he hid from Saul and lived under the strain of constant persecution and pursuit. Reading it today, we can sense the inner turmoil that David knew during that critical time, and we can see reflected feelings we ourselves have known in times of stress.

> I cry with my voice to the Lord,
>   with my voice I make supplication to the
>   Lord,
> I pour out my complaint before him,
>   I tell my trouble before him.
> When my spirit is faint,
>   thou knowest my way!
>
> In the path where I walk
>   they have hidden a trap for me.
> I look to the right and watch,
>   but there is none who takes notice of me;
>   no refuge remains to me,
>   no man cares for me.
>
> I cry to thee, O Lord;
>   I say, Thou art my refuge,
>   my portion in the land of the living.

105

Give heed to my cry;
for I am brought very low!

Deliver me from my persecutors,
for they are too strong for me!
Bring me out of prison,
that I may give thanks to thy name!
The righteous will surround me;
for thou wilt deal bountifully with me.

Psalm 142:1-7 (RSV)

The years of suffering were forging David's character. God was applying pressures to the godly youth that would mature him into a man. David's experiences forced him to plumb the depths of his humanity—and to find that in every extremity God was his only refuge. David often found himself in situations where the temptation to choose the easy way was great. At times David did choose wrongly. But in the great tests—like that moment when he stood over the sleeping Saul—David found the strength to choose what he believed to be God's will. It was this strength, this heart for God, which was at the core of David's developing character. It was this strength which made David great, as it can make you and me.

THE PSALMS

The era of David brings us not only political but also religious and literary revival. Many of the psalms recorded in Scripture came from David's

106

own pen, and many others were written during his reign. In fact, the psalms are so vital to our understanding of David that throughout these next chapters we are forced to interpret his history through insights the psalms give into his inner life.

There are several characteristics of the Book of Psalms which we need to note initially.

Hebrew poetry. Unlike English poetry, which emphasizes rhyme and meter, Hebrew poetry relies on other characteristics for its impact.

1. *Parallelism.* Hebrew poetry repeats and rearranges thoughts (rather than sounds). There are several types of parallel arrangement of thoughts, with three being basic.

- *Synonymous:* The same thought is repeated.
  But God in heaven merely laughs!
  He is amused by all their puny plans.
  Psalm 2:4 (TLB)
- *Anthithetical:* A contrasting thought emphasizes the first.
  The young lions do lack, and suffer hunger;
  But they that seek Jehovah shall not want
      any good thing.
  Psalm 34:10 (ASV)
- *Synthetic:* Following thoughts add to or explain a first expression.
  He is like a tree
      planted by streams of water,
  that yields its fruit in its season,
      and its leaf does not wither.
  Psalm 1:3 (RSV)

107

It is important to recognize parallelism in Hebrew poetry. Our understanding of the text hinges on sensing this thought pattern.

2. *Rhythm.* In the original text, accent marks indicated stress. But this rhythm is not metrical, and is not distinguishable in the English translations.

3. *Figures of speech.* Hebrew poetry, like the Hebrew language itself, uses vivid imagery, similes, and metaphors to communicate thoughts and feelings. These, like parallelism, are easily translated into other languages, though at times their idiomatic use may obscure the full meaning.

When we understand the characteristics of Hebrew poetry, we are quickly able to enter into the pattern and to identify the feelings and emotions the writers convey.

Inner life. Like the poetry of other peoples, Hebrew poetry is not designed so much to communicate information as it is to share the inner life and feelings of its writers.

This characteristic of the Psalms is very important to us, and a dynamic aspect of the divine revelation. Through the Psalms we are able to see the men and women of Scripture as real persons, gripped by the feelings that move us as well. We are also able to sense a relationship with God that is deeply personal and real. Every dimension of the human personality is touched when faith establishes that personal relationship. God meets us as whole persons—He touches our feelings and emotions, our joys and sorrows, our deepest inner needs. Faith in God is not just an intellectual kind of thing; it is a relationship which engages everything that we are. Thus, in the Psalms we have a picture of the relationship to which God is calling us today—a relationship in which we have freedom to be ourselves, and to share ourselves freely with the Lord and other believers.

David stands as one of history's greatest men. In his psalms, David shares himself with us as a *real* man of flesh and blood in his weaknesses and strengths. David's total commitment of himself to God shows us the way to grow toward our own greatness in Christ.

GOING DEEPER
to personalize

1. Read through I Samuel 16—31 as you would a novel.

2. The following chart gives a partial breakdown of David's psalms which may reflect the three stages of his life explored in this chapter. Read these psalms, jotting down any insights they give you into David's growth toward greatness.

Early Years	In Saul's Court	Persecution
Psalm 19	Psalm 59	Psalm 10
23		13
29		27
		34
		142

3. From the above, select the one psalm which most accurately portrays how you feel just now. What experiences have given rise to your feelings? Why not express your feelings to the Lord, using the selected psalm as a prayer or as a model for writing your own prayer.

4. If you had to give titles to your own life stages, what titles would you give them? Phrase your titles to reflect the reason why you see your life as having these particular stages.

5. For an insight into David's feelings after being delivered from Saul, read Psalm 18.

THE KINGDOM COME

WITH THE DEATH OF Saul, David's fortune changed. No longer a fugitive, he was recognized as king by the southern tribe of Judah, his own people. In the north, Ishbosheth, a surviving son of Saul, was propped up as king by the military leader Abner. Over the next years there were minor skirmishes between the two kingdoms, but David's strength showed itself, as did Ishbosheth's weakness. Then Ishbosheth was assassinated (and the assassins executed by an outraged David). Seven and a half years after David had become king of Judah, he became king of all Israel.

David's rule was strong and aggressive and his accomplishments were unparalleled. Other men of history have demonstrated military and administrative capacity, but David overshadows them all by the breadth and depth of his ability. To cap it all, he is one of the great men of faith. To understand the calling of this remarkable man it is necessary to survey his accomplishments and review his significance in Old Testament history and prophecy.

DAVID'S ACCOMPLISHMENTS

Military achievements. Establishing the kingdom first of all required defeating Israel's enemies and setting up a perimeter of safety. As archaeological digs have shown, up to David's time Israel was restricted to the hilly areas of Palestine; the rich plains were in the hands of the ancient Canaanite peoples. Then, in a series of battles (II Sam. 5, 6, 8, 10) David destroyed the power of the Philistines, Israel's principal enemy since the days of Samson. David's neutralization of the Philistines was complete; they never again posed any threat to God's people.

In a further series of battles, David brought Moab and Edom under his control. The kingdom of Israel proper then extended from north of the Sea of Galilee south to Beersheba and encompassed both sides of the Jordan River.

David's conquests set up a number of vassal states which insulated Israel from distant potential enemies. They also made available the natural resources of iron and coke which Israel needed to maintain military strength and the skills in metalworking which were not native in Israel. No longer would iron, the Philistines' ancient "secret weapon," be unavailable to the Hebrews.

Summarizing the position David had attained for

FIGURE VIII   **DAVID'S KINGDOM**

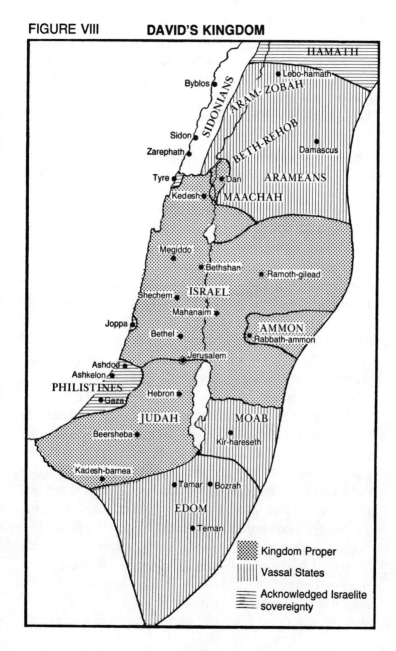

113

Israel, Leon Wood *(A Survey of Israel's History)* notes of all the territory which acknowledged Israelite sovereignty, "this was the area which God had promised to Abraham for his posterity centuries before (Gen. 15:18). It did not rival the vast territories of Egypt, Assyria, Babylonia, et al, in their empire days; but in David's time it was one of the larger land areas held, and David was no doubt the strongest ruler of the contemporary world."

Government organization. David quickly took steps to maintain all military and political gains. He instituted a creative military plan under which 24,000 men were always under arms. The personnel rotated every month, according to I Chronicles 27:1-15, indicating that at least 288,000 trained men were ready for immediate service if needed, and yet able to devote most of their time to civilian pursuits. The core of David's military organization was his 600 key commanders, his *gibborim,* or "mighty men," over whom, in turn, was a smaller general staff.

David's genius for organization showed itself in religious and civil areas as well. While we are not told of their duties, David apparently set a governor over each of the twelve tribal areas and also established a cabinet for the central government. Members' duties included supervision of his treasury, various agricultural departments, etc. (I Chr. 27:25-31).

Centralization. Since the days of Joshua, the people of Israel had thought more in terms of tribal than national identity. This was the reason for David's ready acceptance by Judah, his own tribe, and the slower acceptance by the others. As king over the

114

whole nation, David quickly acted to centralize the government by choosing a suitable site for the capital. He realized both the religious and political significance of affirming Israel's identity as a whole.

The city David selected was occupied at that time by the Jebusites. It was so strongly fortified that its inhabitants boasted that the lame and the blind could defend it against David (II Sam. 5: 6). But David's army took the city by storm, overcoming those "lame and blind" defenders. The city of Jerusalem was located on the border between Judah and the northern tribes—a wise political as well as military choice.

Jerusalem became the capital; and when David moved the Ark of the Covenant to the city, it became the center of the religious life of Israel as well. Through David, God selected that foretold city, "the place which the Lord your God will choose out of all your tribes to put his name and make his habitation there" (Deut. 12: 5, RSV). From that time on, Israel was to offer sacrifice only at Jerusalem and to appear there before the Lord at the time of the three special feasts.

This political and religious unification of the people around a central location and with a recognized central government was one of David's greatest accomplishments, involving as it did a reorientation of the tribal life-style and thought pattern of the people.

Structuring worship. David's genius for organization also showed itself in his impact on Israel's religious life. Zadok and Abiathar served as chief priests[1] and were members of David's cabinet. The priests and the Levites under them were organized into 24 shifts, each called to serve one week at a time at the Jerusalem sanctuary (I Chr. 24: 1-19). Thus, priests and Levites typically served two weeks a year; the rest of the time they lived at their homes. David was also served by prophets, Gad and Nathan, who had a special ministry in instructing (and reproving) the king.

David took a special interest in organizing the singers and musicians who served the Temple (I Chr. 25: 1-31). Many of the psalms which he wrote were used in public worship. His personal commitment was reflected in the fresh interest of Israel in the service of God during the years of his reign.

David's reign was marked by many internal troubles and struggles. He was not always in a position to enforce his will on those with whom he shared power; at other times his own action brought disasters. But David's genius, committed to the service of God and enriched by His Spirit, shaped Israel into a people who knew a brief time of glory under his reign.

Throughout David's life, God's people stood on the pinnacle of long-promised power. In the transition David effected, Israel moved:

1. from government by judges to a monarchy

[1] Abiathar's son, Ahimelech, served in the office of high priest with Zadok after Abiathar's death (see I Chr. 18: 16). There is some uncertainty as to why there were two high priests, but it may have been due to political reasons. See a resource such as *Unger's Bible Dictionary* for more in-depth treatment.

2. from anarchy to a strong centralized government
3. from a loose confederation of tribes to a unified nation
4. from poverty and Bronze Age technology to an iron economy and wealth
5. from being a subject people to becoming conquerors
6. from decentralized to centralized worship

This transformation was God's work through David, and stands as a portrait of what we can expect to see under our own coming King.

THE BIBLICAL RECORD

David's history is recorded in two complementary sets of Old Testament narrative books. First and II Samuel are a contemporary record, probably begun by Samuel himself and completed by Nathan and Gad (I Chr. 29: 29). The other set of books covering David's life is the Chronicles, written during the Captivity after Judah had been destroyed and the people carried to Babylon (see I Chr. 1-9). These books cover the same ground (see "overlap" chart on the next page), but the material is treated from a different viewpoint with distinctly different purposes.

Whereas I and II Samuel set out to show the establishment of the Old Testament Kingdom of God, I and II Chronicles set out to chronicle the entire sacred history from Adam to the day of the writer. With such a massive subject, selectivity is

117

FIGURE IX

TEMPORAL OVERLAP CHART

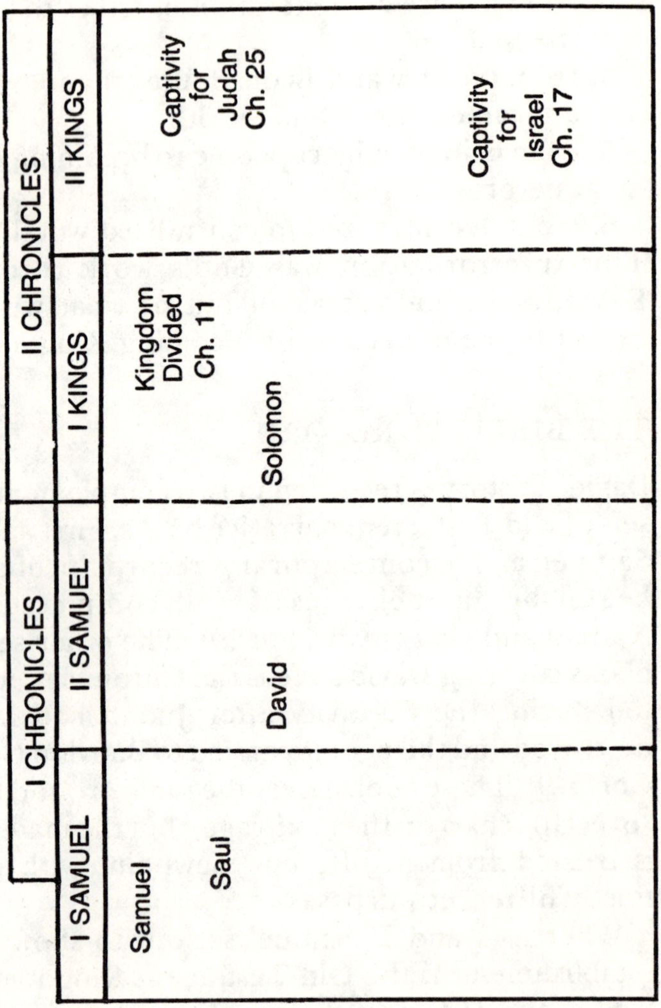

	I CHRONICLES		II CHRONICLES	
I SAMUEL	II SAMUEL	I KINGS	II KINGS	
Samuel				
Saul				
	David			
		Solomon		
		Kingdom Divided Ch. 11		
			Captivity for Judah Ch. 25	
			Captivity for Israel Ch. 17	

118

the key, and the chronicler zooms through the ages to focus on the Davidic line and Temple worship. Israel's evil kings are only mentioned where they come in contact with Judah, and even the discussion of the Davidic line focuses on the good kings.

The Chronicles are, then, essentially a theological overview of history. They were written after the Exile, when Israel had fallen into such sin that they were expelled from the Promised Land. The glory of David's day was remembered but had long faded. The divine commentary in these books recalls the glory, not as a lost dream, but as evidence that God fulfills His commitments to His people and will yet fulfill His promise of an everlasting Kingdom.

THE EVERLASTING KINGDOM

David has prophetic as well as historic significance. When the kingdom of Israel had been firmly established, David yearned to build a suitable temple for the Lord. But David was not permitted to build that house. Instead, God spoke to him (II Sam. 7:12-16) and promised to build *him* a house (i.e., establish a dynasty)!

David was promised that after his death a descendant of his would be established as ruler of a kingdom to be set up in God's name. God promised, "I will establish the throne of his kingdom for ever" (II Sam. 7:13, RSV). David's line was promised the perpetual right to Israel's throne even

119

though David's immediate descendant, Solomon, sinned in such terrible ways that he deserved to be set aside. But because of David's faith, God did not treat his descendants as he had Saul. Sin would be punished, but David's line would never be cut off completely.

God's promise to David is recognized in the Old and the New Testaments as an amplification of the original Abrahamic Covenant. It explains the means through which the promise to Abraham would be fulfilled. As Psalm 89: 3, 4 (RSV) expresses it,

> Thou hast said, "I have made a covenant with
>   my chosen one,
>   I have sworn to David my servant:
> 'I will establish your descendants for ever,
>   and build your throne for all generations.'"

From that point on, for the Hebrew people and later prophets, David stood as the symbol and the ancestor of a coming King destined to set up a lasting Kingdom through which the whole world would be related to God (see especially Jer. 33: 22, 25, 26). God's formal promise was confirmed over and over again in such passages as Isaiah 9: 6, 7; Jeremiah 23: 5, 6; 30: 8, 9; 33: 14-17, 20, 21; Ezekiel 37: 24, 25; Daniel 7: 13, 14; Hosea 3: 4, 5; Amos 9: 11; and Zechariah 14: 3, 9. We cannot understand the Old Testament or the hope with which godly Jews looked forward to the coming Messiah if we do not realize that they looked for a literal kingdom on earth, to be established and ruled over for an endless age by David's greater Son.

No wonder New Testament writers took such pains to demonstrate that Jesus of Nazareth is David's descendant, and thus genealogically qualified to mount his throne. We can also understand the confusion which arose when Jesus did not repeat David's military and political performance! Rather than throwing off the yoke of Rome as David had thrown off the yoke of the Philistines, Jesus bowed His head and let Himself be led away and crucified. He who could have called on angel armies to release Him chose instead the shameful death of the cross.

Even after Jesus' resurrection, His disciples could not understand what had happened. They are recorded in Acts to have asked him, "Lord, are you at this time going to restore the kingdom to Israel?" (1: 6, NIV). Certainly God's rule of the universe and over the ages is recognized in both the Old and New Testaments. But these men were concerned about that form of the overarching rule of God known not as the "kingdom" but as "the kingdom promised to Israel!" As Jews they were curious about the destiny of their own nation.

Christ's answer was no rebuke. The promises God has made will be fulfilled. So Jesus simply said, "It is not for you to know the times or dates" (Acts 1: 7, NIV). In Jesus, men of faith had correctly seen David's descendant who would one day establish an endless earthly kingdom. But they had not seen the centuries which lay between Jesus' first coming with His suffering as man's Savior, and His still future Second Coming as Israel's— and the earth's—King.

It is important that *we* see Him as the coming King. Right now He is the Savior to us, and our Lord as well. But the day is coming when Jesus will be *Lord of all.* The careening course of modern history, rushing as it seems to be toward disasters over which men have no control, points up our need to reaffirm the fact that history has a goal. This very earth, the setting of man's first sin, will once again know the masterful touch of God's own hand. "I will tell of the decree of the Lord," says the psalmist of that future day.

> He said to me, "You are my son,
>   today I have begotten you.
> Ask of me, and I will make the nations your
>   heritage,
>   and the ends of the earth your possession.
> You shall break them with a rod of iron,
>   and dash them in pieces like a potter's ves-
>   sel."
>
> *Psalm 2: 7-9 (RSV)*

The Old Testament picture of David, acting in his own might to establish Israel's glorious kingdom, is but a dim foreshadowing of David's son, Jesus Christ, who will come again to act in even greater power and to establish a worldwide Kingdom whose glory knows no end.

122

GOING DEEPER
to personalize

1. Read I Chronicles 10-28 for the divine commentary on the Davidic period.

2. Look over these psalms, which are prophetic in character and foreshadow events associated with Christ's coming as King:

Psalm 45: a love song addressed to the King

Psalm 46: a portrait of the tribulation time during which all will be brought under the King's authority

Psalm 47: a word picture of the joy the earth will experience under Christ's rule

Psalm 48: praise to God who has finally filled all His promises

to probe

1. There are many aspects of the Davidic period which merit extended study. Below are several topics which might be explored by direct study of the Scriptures involved or by using resource books discussing this period. (One fine set of books is *The Zondervan Pictorial Encyclopedia of the Bible.*)

Select at least one of these topics to examine:

a) David's conquests: II Samuel 5, 6, 8, 10; I Chronicles 18-20.

b) David's capital: I Chronicles 13, 15, 17.

c) Prophetic significance of Jerusalem (Zion): see concordance.

d) David's army: II Samuel 18, 23; I Chronicles 11, 27.

    e) David's administration: I Chronicles 27;
      II Samuel 8, 20.
    f) David's religious reforms: I Chronicles 24, 25.
    g) The Davidic covenant: see text, pp. 119, 120
      for references.
    h) New Testament references to David: see con-
      cordance.

2. A detailed examination of Old Testament prophecy can be found in the fifth book of this **Bible Alive Series.** However, you might wish to look at Matthew 5 and 6 as the constitution of the Kingdom which Jesus will institute. The Sermon on the Mount does give us moral guidance now and shows us, as did the Law, God's character and will for us. Yet, the sermon gives more than individual guidance. It actually describes the life-style which will be dominant under the coming King.

SAINT AND SINNER

FEET OF CLAY. So often it's crushing for us to discover that a person we admire has faults. An idealized parent disappoints. A friend we respect falls short. A political leader we support suffers his own particular Watergate. Discouraged and hurt, we feel a bitterness that is hard to overcome.

When we look in the Biblical record at David, certainly one of history's exceptional men and one whose faith is mentioned in both Testaments, we discover that he, too, had feet of clay. The saint is revealed as a sinner. And we wonder, "Why does God hold up as examples men and women who have such obvious flaws?"

A look at David's life suggests a number of possible answers, some more satisfying than others. For one thing, through David we are reminded that God is a realist. His book contains no "let's pretend" whitewash of believers. Noting this, we may be helped to appreciate the fact that we can come to this God in spite of our own weaknesses. God won't overlook them. But He won't be crushed by our failures either. God knows that "we are dust" (Ps. 103: 14).

For another thing, the revelation of saints' failures as well as successes helps us to identify with them. If a David or an Abraham were represented as spiritually perfect, you and I would hardly feel close or similar to him. The truths that God is teaching us through their lives might be seen but might not be felt as relevant. After all, we might think, "That's all right for a spiritual giant like David! But what about poor struggling me?" Then we discover that David struggled too. And sometimes he lost out to his sin nature. David did know sin's pull just as we do; his experiences *are* relevant to us.

The new Testament affirms, "There hath no temptation taken you but such as is common to man" (I Cor. 10: 13). We are all bound up together in the shared ties of humanity. David knew the feelings and temptations that you know—and you know his! When the Bible accurately reports the failures and follies of God's saints, it demonstrates this common bond and encourages us to identify our own inner struggles with theirs.

Most importantly, when Old Testament saints are shown to be sinners, Scripture is expressing something basic about the Gospel. The good news of God's love for man is not "Trust me, and be perfect." The good news of God's love is that the

126

Lord has committed Himself to deal with sin and to make us progressively more and more like Him. For progressive growth we always stand in need of God's grace and aid. God deals with sin by the means of forgiveness. The greatness of David is not in his perfection but in his willingness to face his sin and to return wholeheartedly to God.

How different from Saul. When Saul sinned, he begged Samuel to stay with him, that the people might not discover God's anger. When the prophet Nathan confronted David concerning his sin with Bathsheba, David not only confessed immediately, but he even wrote a psalm used later in public worship, openly admitting his fault and sharing the inner anguish that accompanied loss of fellowship with God!

We cannot, and God did not, condone David's sins and failings. But we can praise God for moving David to share honestly with us. Through David we learn fresh lessons about the grace of God, and we are reminded that you and I are invited to come boldly to the Lord, too, that He may meet us—and our needs.

DAVID AND BATHSHEBA
II Samuel 11, 12

This familiar story recalls a time when David was in Jerusalem rather than with his campaigning armies. From the roof of his palace, David noticed a beautiful woman bathing, and he sent for her. When she became pregnant, he ordered her husband Uriah home from the front so the adultery might not be discovered. But Uriah was a dedicated man; he would not enjoy the comforts of his home or wife while his companions camped in the open before the walls of the enemy city.

Desperate now, David sent secret orders to his commander to place Uriah in an exposed position so the enemy might kill him. After Uriah's death, Bathsheba was taken into David's house as one of his wives. And the Bible tells us, "What David had done was wrong in the eyes of the Lord" (II Sam. 11:27, NEB).

Now came a confrontation between David and Nathan the prophet, who was sent to announce God's judgment on the king. David had violated the sanctity of the home; his own home now would produce evil. This judgment needs to be seen as a natural consequence of David's act; his own disrespect for the divinely ordained family pattern would bear its own bitter fruit.

David's immediate reaction is revealing. Unlike others, who struck out in anger against the prophets who condemned them, David confessed his sin and admitted the rightness of God's judgment: "David said to Nathan, 'I have sinned against the Lord'" (12:13, RSV).

David's confession brought him forgiveness. But it could not change the course of events his choices had set in motion. David would not die, but his child would. One day David would go to be with the son whom the Lord had taken, but that son would never know David on earth (12:23).

Scripture tells this story simply. All the facts are recorded. No cover-up is attempted. Meditating on the incident, David was led to make the fullest possible revelation of his inner thoughts and feelings. We find them in Psalm 51, a psalm later used in public worship. We see timeless themes in Psalm 51, guidance to help us realize how we ourselves are to approach God when we sin. As the analysis of this psalm on the following pages shows, David's reaction is appropriate for us too when we sin.

THE PENITENT'S PSALM

A plea for mercy
>Have mercy on me, O God,
>   according to thy steadfast love;
>according to thy abundant mercy
>   blot out my transgressions.
>Wash me thoroughly from my iniquity,
>   and cleanse me from my sin!

Admission of guilt
>For I know my transgressions,
>   and my sin is ever before me.
>Against thee, thee only, have I sinned,
>   and done that which is evil in thy sight,
>   so that thou art justified in thy sentence
>   and blameless in thy judgment.
>Behold, I was brought forth in iniquity,
>   and in sin did my mother conceive me.

Forgiveness and cleansing needed
>Behold, thou desirest truth in the inward be-
>   ing;

therefore teach me wisdom in my secret
heart.
Purge me with hyssop, and I shall be clean;
wash me, and I shall be whiter than snow.
Fill me with joy and gladness;
let the bones which thou hast broken rejoice.
Hide thy face from my sins,
and blot out all my iniquities.

Forgiveness will lead to restoration of fellowship
Create in me a clean heart, O God,
and put a new and right spirit within me.
Cast me not away from thy presence,
and take not thy holy Spirit from me.
Restore to me the joy of thy salvation,
and uphold me with a willing spirit.

*Future ministry depends on God's forgiveness and en-
ablement*
Then I will teach transgressors thy ways,
and sinners will return to thee.
Deliver me from bloodguiltiness, O God,
thou God of my salvation,
and my tongue will sing aloud of thy deliverance.

*Full and willing heart submission is recognized as God's
prime concern*
O Lord, open thou my lips,
and my mouth shall show forth thy praise.
For thou hast no delight in sacrifice;
were I to give a burnt offering,
thou wouldst not be pleased.

> The sacrifice acceptable to God is a broken
>   spirit;
> A broken and contrite heart, O
> God, thou wilt not despise.
>
> *Psalm 51 (RSV)*

David had penetrated to the heart of the issue. His was no legal relationship with some "book-keeper God" who cares only about balanced books. David did not rush to ask what he could do for God to make up for his sin! Instead David realized that God's concern is *personal* rather than *legal* in nature. A contrite heart means more to God than all anyone might possibly do for Him.

With David's heart attitude corrected, forgiveness could flow and the Spirit of God work again to cleanse David. Cleansed, God would work through David to do good for Zion and for all His people.

ABSALOM'S REVOLT

II Samuel 13-19

David's children shared his weaknesses, but few demonstrated his redeeming characteristic of contriteness. David's life-style was one of responsiveness to God; in his infrequent departures, David was open to correction.

Not so his sons. In these chapters, we read of one son, Amnon, who seduced a half sister and then spurned her. The girl's brother, Absalom, plotted revenge and later killed Amnon. This son, Absalom, was then banished. Later, through the influence of David's general, Joab, the banishment was lifted, but David refused to see Absalom.

David had two possible courses open here: the execution of Absalom for murder, or restoration through confession and forgiveness. David took neither course. Absalom's sin, undealt with, festered within his personality.

In time Absalom began a careful campaign to woo the tribes of Israel and to alienate them from David. Amazingly, he succeeded! The tribes of Israel (those who had been last to crown David king some decades before) swung their support to Absalom who, after having himself crowned, marched on Jerusalem. David was forced to flee for his life from the capital, with only his old companions remaining faithful—plus a band of mercenary soldiers whom he had employed for his personal guard just the day before! How deeply it must have cut him to see these mercenaries remain true to their commitment while his own people spurned him.

II Samuel 13-19 traces the origin and the course of the rebellion and reveals something of David's own doubt and discouragement. Without question, David examined himself and found many reasons why the Lord might be justified in removing him from his throne.

David fled toward Judah, aided by a few individuals. In the meantime David's supporters in Zion gave bad advice to Absalom, which allowed David time to gather an army from his homeland.

In the battle which followed, Absalom was killed—against David's orders.

The story ends with David crying out in agony and weeping over the lost son.

This experience was one of wrenching pain for David, and again his innermost thoughts and feelings are shared with us in the Psalms. Psalm 3 emerges from the time of self-examination and self-doubt as David fled Jerusalem. It is short, yet its simple phrases take us deep into David's heart and show us how he handled one of those times which we all experience: a time when everything goes wrong and all seems hopeless.

Implications of the rebellion. David saw clearly that the fact of rebellion indicated that his people believed that God was no longer for him. He was forced to examine that question and recognized a certain justification for the accusation of Shimei that David was a "man of blood."

> O Lord, how many are my foes!
> Many are rising against me;
>> many are saying of me,
>>> there is no help for him in God.
>
> *Selah*[1]
> *Psalm 3:1*

Remembrance of God's past role in David's life. With his world tumbling down, David looked to God and characterized the relationship he had enjoyed

[1]*Selah* may be a musical notation, indicating rest or pause. When it appears in the Psalms, it suggests stopping to meditate on a completed thought.

133

with the Lord across the years. Each believer's past experience of God's blessing and lessons learned about the character of the Lord are a comfort when things go wrong.

Specifically David thought of God as his protector and strengthener (the "lifter of my head"). Even more significantly, David called God "my glory." The earthly glory David attained—his status and wealth as Israel's king—were empty things to him. It was God and God alone in whom David gloried. David's final thought before another meditative pause focused on God as one who answers prayer.

> But thou, O Lord, art a shield about me,
>   my glory, and the lifter of my head.
> I cry aloud to the Lord,
>   and he answers me from his holy hill.
>
> *Selah*
> *Psalm 3:3, 4*

Release from tension comes by turning it over to God. Then comes a striking revelation of David's commitment of himself to God. He lay down and went to sleep. Neither self-doubt nor anguish nor fear could hold him in its grip. Certainly David felt all of these emotions. Yet, by focusing his attention on the Lord and who He is, life was put in perspective and David was freed to rest.

> I lie down and sleep;
>   I wake again, for the Lord sustains me.

I am not afraid of ten thousands of people
   who have set themselves against me round
   about.

Psalm 3:5, 6

Such trust is not fatalism. One Stoic philosopher, a slave, is said to have been beaten and mistreated by his master. On one occasion when the master was twisting his leg, the Stoic warned, "If you keep on twisting my leg you'll break it." The sadistic master maintained the pressure, and the leg snapped. The Stoic's only remark was, "See, I told you it would break."

David was hardly such a person. Neither are you and I. To say that we trust in God and rest in Him never means that we do not care. And so we hear David give a last passionate cry, and trust the outcome to his God of deliverance.

Arise, O Lord!
   Deliver me, O my God!
For thou dost smite all my enemies on the
   cheek,
   thou dost break the teeth of the wicked.
Deliverance belongs to the Lord;
   thy blessing be upon thy people!

Selah
Psalm 3:7, 8 (RSV)

THE GODLY MAN

It is easy to emphasize one side of David's character at the expense of the other. Some tend to idealize David and attempt to explain away his faults. Yet David had many weaknesses. Others are horrified by the cruelty and selfishness he showed when he took Bathsheba and arranged for her husband's "accident." They cannot reconcile this behavior with the brave and trusting shepherd boy, or the man who flung aside his dignity with his royal robes to dance in joy before the Lord, or with the youth whose days as a shepherd taught him to view God as man's Shepherd and who shares this beautiful insight with us in Psalm 23. Somehow we feel uncomfortable in the presence of a man who is both a sinner and a saint.

Yet, strikingly, David is portrayed as a man approved by God: one whose heart Scripture says was "faithful to the Lord" (I Ki. 15: 3, NEB). David thus stands before us as a unique example of how sin distorts the best of men, and how the best of men deal with sin in contrition and confession.

Even more, David stands before us as a testimony to God's love and His goodness. God's grace touched David. He forgave David's sins and enabled him for the task to which he was called.

How wonderful to realize that God yearns to deal with us this same way. For our sins, He has provided through Jesus Christ a full and free forgiveness, one that blots out the past and opens up the future as well. Through the Holy Spirit who has come to dwell within, God has provided strength to enable us to meet life's challenges, fully equipping us for whatever life to which you and I are called.

GOING DEEPER
to personalize

1. Jot down (for yourself, not to share with others) details about a time recently when you failed to do what was right and became aware of your sin. Include how you felt and what you did.

Then compare your experience with Psalm 51 and Psalm 32, each of which is a psalm of confession. How do your experience and these psalms compare? Contrast?

2. From Psalms 32 and 51, write down a procedure to follow when you find yourself in a similar situation again. It is wonderful to realize that God *has* made a way for us to deal with our sin!

3. Study thoroughly the events recorded in II Samuel 13—19, and then reread Psalms 3 and 4.

4. Use a concordance and check the occurrence of the word *glory* in David's psalms. From this study, what do you conclude about David's personal value system?

to probe

1. Do a time line of David's life, listing all the major events and periods of his life, from shepherd boy on through his years as king. Then read each of the psalms ascribed to David, and place each in a period of his life from which the psalm might have sprung.

2. Develop a comparative study analyzing Saul and David. Show why David was a "man after God's own heart" while Saul definitely was not.

THE PSALMS FOR TODAY

IN THE LAST CHAPTERS we've often looked to the Book of Psalms to give us insights into David's reactions in the critical experiences of his life. David's psalms have helped us know him as a real person, not just another distant great man of history.

This ability to express the reality of human experience is one of the great distinctives of the Psalms. Dr. Samuel Schultz in *The Old Testament Speaks* notes that "they express the common experience of the human race. Composed by numerous authors, the various psalms express the emotions, personal feelings, attitudes, gratitude, and interests of the average individual. Universally people have identified their lot in life with that of the psalmist." In every experience of our own, no matter how deep the pain or great the frustration or exhilarating the joy, we can find psalms which echo our inmost being, psalms which God uses to bring comfort or confirm release.

This real-life characteristic of the Psalms is at the root of several of their greatest values to us and the ground for some of the most unique and potent messages of the Word.

PERSONAL MESSAGES FROM PSALMS

There are three personal messages we hear in Psalms more clearly than in any other section of Scripture.

(1) *It's all right to be human.* The Bible tells us that in Creation God viewed man, the culmination of His creative work, and affirmed His work as "very good" (Gen. 1: 31). Man, the Bible says, is made in God's image, and we are taught to value our humanity. As persons we share a certain likeness to Him.

Sometimes, aware that sin has entered the race and warped mankind out of the divinely intended pattern, we come to view our humanity with shame and guilt instead of pride. A person who tends to locate the identity of man in his character as sinner rather than in his nature as one in the image of God is likely to repress his human feelings and emotions. Struggling for "control," he may be uncomfortable with strong feelings and attempt to hold them in or to deny them.

The Bible really does teach us to affirm our value and worth as human beings, not to deny our humanity. Psalm 8 speaks in wonder that God

140

should have created man "a little lower than the angels" and "crowned him with glory and honour." Hebrews 2:10 echoes the thought that we are never to let slip the awareness that God's intention in Christ was to bring "many sons to glory." Christ calls Himself our brother; He was "made like His brethren in all things" (2:17, NASB). Far from being ashamed of his humanity, the Christian is free to rejoice in who he is, knowing that in Creation and in redemption God has affirmed his worth.

Such teaching passages might help us grasp this affirmation about man intellectually. But we are gripped by it when we read the Psalms! For here we see our own inner experiences openly shared without shame or hesitation, and we discover that God values man's inner life enough to record this dynamic record of it in His own Word.

When we read the psalms and see in them our own emotions and struggles, we find a great release. We hear their message clearly now. It *is* all right to be human. It *is* all right to be ourselves. We need not fear what is within us or repress the feeling side of life.

(2) *There's a way out.* One reason why emotions frighten us is that many people do not know how to express or release them. In our culture, the recognition and expression of feelings are not encouraged—especially of negative feelings. Feelings are feared. To feel anger welling up within and to sense that we're on the verge of losing control is a frightening thing.

141

For Christians there is also the awful notion that it is wrong to feel fear or anger or tension. *If only I were a good Christian,* we're liable to tell ourselves. *If only I were really trusting in the Lord.* So we feel guilt over the emotions that touch us, and then all too often we try to deny this very important aspect of being a person.

Reading the psalms carefully, we often trace a process in which the writer begins with strong and almost uncontrollable feelings. We see how he struggles with them, and we see how he brings his feelings to God or relates them to what He knows of the Lord and His ways. In reading Psalms, you and I can learn how to handle our own emotions creatively and how to relate feelings to faith.

Psalm 73 is a good example of this "working through" process. It begins with the writer confessing that he had become envious of the wicked—certainly not an unusual experience when we are facing difficulties ourselves and then see everything apparently going well for the man or woman who cared nothing for God.

> I was envious of the arrogant,
>> when I saw the prosperity of the wicked.
> For they have no pangs;
>> their bodies are sound and sleek.
> They are not in trouble as other men are;
>> they are not stricken like other men.
> Therefore pride is their necklace;
>> violence covers them as a garment.

. . . .

And they say, "How can God know?
  Is there knowledge in the Most High?"
Behold, these are the wicked;
  always at ease, they increase in riches.
All in vain have I kept my heart clean
  and washed my hands in innocence.
For all day long I have been stricken,
  and chastened every morning.
Psalm 73:3-14

How hard it seemed! What good was it to be good? Frustration, envy, self-pity—all have griped Asaph, the Levite who wrote this psalm, and who now faces rather than represses his inner state.

The passage goes on to explain how the writer handled these feelings. First of all, he tried to think the problem through, but "it seemed to me a wearisome task" (v. 16). He went to God with his problem, to pray at His sanctuary. There God gave him an answer. Asaph's thoughts were directed to the end toward which the sinner's life leads.

Truly thou dost set them in slippery places;
  thou dost make them fall to ruin.
How they are destroyed in a moment,
  swept away utterly by terrors!
They are like a dream when one awakes,
  on awaking you despise their phantoms.
Psalm 73:18-20

The easy life of the scoffers had led them to forget God, and their success had not permitted them to sense their need of Him. The very wealth and ease which Asaph had envied were "slippery places" Asaph's own trials helped him avoid.

This new perspective changed Asaph's feelings. His past feelings were "stupid and ignorant, I was like a beast toward thee" (v. 22). His emotional reactions in this case had not corresponded with reality. Yet, when God showed Asaph reality, his emotions changed.

> Nevertheless I am continually with thee;
>   thou dost hold my right hand.
> Thou dost guide me with thy counsel,
>   and afterward thou wilt receive me to glory.
> Whom have I in heaven but thee?
>   And there is nothing upon earth that I de-
>   sire besides thee.
> My flesh and my heart may fail,
>   but God is the strength of my heart and my
>   portion for ever.
>
> *Psalm 73:23-26 (RSV)*

Real life always holds such struggles for us. There is nothing wrong with them. Our emotions are not bad; they are part of being a human being. The glory of the believer's privilege is that, because he knows God, his emotions can be brought into fullest harmony with reality. You and I can face all of our feelings—and find freedom to be ourselves with the Lord. What a privilege to be ourselves with the Lord and experience His gentle transformation.

(3) *We can be honest with God.* This is a third great message of Psalms. Just as we need not repress our feelings, we need not try to hide our feelings from God. He loves us and accepts us as we are—yet always so creatively that we are freed to grow toward all that we want to become.

How freeing to realize that God's love is unconditional. He is concerned about every aspect of our life, inviting us to share all that we are with Him, that in return He might share Himself with us and bring us to health and wholeness.

WORSHIP

While the Psalms tell us much about ourselves, they are also of great benefit in their revelation of God as they guide us into worship.

Classifications of Psalms. There are many ways in which commentators have attempted to classify the Psalms. One approach is by content: analysis of the themes which seem to recur. For instance, there are a number of *Messianic psalms* that speak about Christ. There are *Imprecatory psalms* in which judgment is called for against enemies. There are psalms of praise and penitence and worship. Such classification systems help us categorize the psalms individually, but they do not help us in organizing the book as a whole.

Actually, we probably shouldn't expect to find a careful or logical structure to the Bible's collection of psalms. Life is complex, filled with surges of joy and contrasting times of stagnant depression, en-

145

riched by the worship of God and yet often strained by difficulty and despair. The Book of Psalms shares the complexity of life itself, reflecting in organization as well as content the nature of human experience.

Yet, one way of classifying the Psalms is of special interest. It is a classification by use. For instance, many psalms have titles, such as *mizmor* or *shir*. These words refer to ways that the psalm was integrated into the life and worship of Israel. The 57 psalms entitled *mizmor* were sung to the accompaniment of stringed instruments and were probably used as public worship songs. There are thirty *shir*, a word meaning secular or sacred song. Other psalms, such as *ma'aloth* (songs of ascent) were sung by pilgrims on the way to Jerusalem for the three compulsory annual feasts (Pss. 120—34).

Simply noting the title may not be of great value in understanding individual psalms. Yet, together the titles give us an engaging picture of the use of these psalms by Israel and a suggestion for their use in our own day. The titles recall a picture sketched by one of the sons of Korah (a Levitical group dedicated to Temple musicianship).

These things I remember,
as I pour out my soul:
how I went with the throng,
and led them in procession to the house of
God,
with glad shouts and songs of thanksgiving,
a multitude keeping festival.

Psalm 42: 4 (RSV)

146

Perhaps this is the chief picture we ought to keep in mind as we approach the Book of Psalms today. Keeping festival, with praise and rejoicing to our God.

Keeping festival This is one of the lost arts of believers, who are called to celebrate their relationship with God. Such celebration comes not because of our feelings alone, but it comes when we realize just who God is and all that He means for us.

One contemporary definition of worship, suggested by Chicago pastor David Mains, helps us focus on a secret of keeping festival. Worship, says Pastor Mains, is essentially "ascribing worth to God for who He by nature is." At heart, then, worship is focusing our attention on the Lord and praising Him for one of those qualities or characteristics of His which sets Him apart in perfection and glory.

There are many psalms which give us insights into how to worship. For instance, each of Psalms 93 through 99 selects a quality of God to emphasize and for which to praise Him. In Psalm 95, the writer is taken up with the greatness of God and calls all men to worship Him and respond to Him:

O come, let us sing to the Lord;
  let us make a joyful noise to the rock of our
    salvation!
Let us come into his presence with thanksgiving;

147

> let us make a joyful noise to him with songs
>   of praise!
> For the Lord is a great God,
>   and a great King above all gods.
> In his hand are the depths of the earth;
>   the heights of the mountains are his also.
> The sea is his, for he made it;
>   for his hands formed the dry land.
> O come, let us worship and bow down,
>   let us kneel before the Lord, our Maker!
> For he is our God,
>   and we are the people of his pasture,
>   and the sheep of his hand.
>
> *Psalm 95:1-7 (RSV)*

Lifted up, our own eyes are given a fresh vision of who God is, and our spirits are borne along with the psalmist's as we give God our own heart's praise as well.

This sequence of short psalms helps us see what a rich potential there is for worship in contemplation of God and His qualities.

Psalm 93 praises God as the reigning King:

> The Lord is king; he is clothed in majesty;
>   the Lord clothes himself with might and
>   fastens on his belt of wrath.
> Thou hast fixed the earth immovable and
>   firm,
>   thy throne firm from of old;
>   from all eternity thou art God.
>
> *Psalm 93:1, 2 (NEB)*

148

Psalm 94 praises God as the One who acts in justice and vengeance:

> O Lord, thou God of vengeance,
>   thou God of vengeance, shine forth!
> Rise up, O judge of the earth;
>   render to the proud their deserts!
> O Lord, how long shall the wicked,
>   how long shall the wicked exult?
>
> *Psalm 94:1-3 (RSV)*

In Psalm 96 the focus is on God as Savior:

> Sing a new song to the Lord;
>   sing to the Lord, all the earth!
> Sing to the Lord, bless His name;
>   proclaim His salvation from day to day.
> Publish His glory among the nations,
>   His marvelous works among all peoples!
>
> *Psalm 96: 1-3 (MLB)*

And so we can go on and on. For our God *is* splendid. We never reach an end of probing His nature and discovering in Him that which calls forth our praise.

It is in the psalmist's clear focus on the person of God that the deepest meaning of this book of Scripture is to be found.

THE PSALMS FOR TODAY

Probably the greatest value of this enriching book

to believers today is found in the pattern it reveals for our inner personal and spiritual life.

Each of us needs models and examples. If we are to learn golf or tennis, we need someone to *show* us how to play—not just to tell us. If we are to learn to love, we need people close to us to teach us how to love by loving. The model, who helps us pattern our own lives by giving, is a powerful positive example and is vital in all human development.

In the Psalms we have such a model.

We can immerse ourselves in the Psalms, and as we do we'll learn ways to express and creatively handle our own emotions and inner needs.

We can come to the Psalms and let them lift our eyes to God and tune our hearts to sing His praise. And as we do we will be learning how to worship.

How great our need is in these two areas! We are human. Our inner life is real—and that inner life can grow and become truly rich as we open ourselves up to God. We are human. Created in God's image, we must always look beyond ourselves to Him to find life's fullest meaning. As our hearts and minds and emotions also become filled with love for God and appreciation of who He is, we will reach out to grasp our unique heritage in the Lord—and to realize something of our eternal destiny as His sons.

GOING DEEPER
to personalize

   1. Jot down one or two emotions you've felt

deeply recently. These may be positive (joy, thankfulness, etc.) or negative (anger, loneliness, envy, etc.). Then scan the Book of Psalms to see if you can locate several instances in which the writer shares your feelings.

2. Study the psalms you located (in No. 1 above). Jot down everything you see there that gives you insight into yourself, into how to handle and express feelings, into truths about God which help you deal with situations which give rise to those feelings with which you are uncomfortable.

Summarize your findings in a two- to three-page paper.

3. One worship psalm which mentions a number of characteristics of God for which to praise Him is Psalm 103. Read it carefully, and make a list of each of God's qualities for which He might be praised.

4. Take one of the qualities listed in No. 3 above, and write your own "praise psalm," organizing it to ascribe worth to God for the fact that He possesses the quality you have chosen.

to probe

1. Check a resource book such as *The Zondervan Pictorial Encyclopedia of the Bible,* and find out everything you can about the Psalms.

2. Make a thorough study of either (a) one emotion and see how it is dealt with in the Psalms, or (b) one classification of the Psalms (such as *imprecatory)* and see what it teaches. Summarize your findings in a four- or five-page paper.

3. A number of books have been written recently about Christians and their emotional problems and needs. Survey two of these books and find out (a) how much—if any—they draw on the Psalms, and how the Psalms are used in them, and (b) if what they say seems to be in harmony with the tone of the Psalms. Again, summarize your findings in a four- or five-page paper.

FROM GLORY TO GLORY: SOLOMON'S KINGDOM

FOR SOME 33 YEARS David aggressively guided Israel to empire status.

But as David grew older, his powers waned. Eventually, a very natural dispute arose over the succession to the throne.

God had earlier revealed to David that He had chosen Solomon to succeed him (see I Chr. 22: 9, 10). David had communicated this to Bathsheba, Solomon's mother (I Ki. 1: 13, 17) and even announced it to the nation (I Chr. 22: 5; 29: 1). Still, Solomon was the sixth of David's living sons; no wonder his older brothers disputed his rights.

As I Kings 1 reports, David's now oldest son, Adonijah, called together most of the key men in Israel with the intention of proclaiming himself king. However, Nathan the prophet and Bathsheba rushed to David. The king acted immediately; he had Solomon proclaimed co-regent.

Adonijah's party was close enough to the city to hear the horns blowing and the shouts of celebration. When word came that David had proclaimed Solomon king, Adonijah's supporters quickly deserted him, and Adonijah hurried to the sacrificial altar to claim sanctuary. Adonijah's life was spared at this time, and Solomon was securely placed on David's throne.

THE SOLOMONIC ERA
I Kings 1–10; II Chronicles 1–9

The years of Solomon's long reign seem to be years of growing glory for Israel. The traditional powers of the ancient world, the Egyptians and the Hittites, and the empires yet to appear, Assyria and Babylon, were not aggressive during either David's or Solomon's reign. David had expanded Israel's sphere of influence by war. Solomon was a diplomat who held what his father had gained. During Solomon's reign, Israel's wealth and power were unmatched.

Strength for peace. One of Solomon's strategies for maintaining peace was to constantly strengthen Israel's military capacity. Like strategists in our day, Solomon wanted to deal with world problems through diplomacy, but he wanted to negotiate from a position of strength rather than weakness. He fortified key cities on the perimeter of Israel's territory and set up outer command posts to give early warning of possible enemy military buildups. In addition, Solomon developed a strong and mobile strike force, assembling some 1,400 chariots and 12,000 horsemen and building stables for 4,000 horses. Solomon's chariot cities have been excavated and indicate the extent of the large standing army he maintained.

This military readiness placed a heavy drain on the kingdom's financial resources. But throughout the years of Solomon's reign, Israel had peace.

Diplomacy. David had won the respect of the great powers surrounding Israel. Solomon now moved to make alliances with them. His many marriages to foreign women were part of this diplomatic strategy; such marriages in that day were a normal way to seal an international alliance. Solomon's marriage to Pharaoh's daughter (I Ki. 3: 1) shows the place Israel had won in the ancient world, as Egypt was a major world power.

Solomon also developed close ties with Hiram I, the Phoenician king of Tyre (c. 978-944). Again, marriage sealed the alliance. But trade between the two powers, with Tyre contributing her "cedars of Lebanon" and Israel providing wheat plus other foodstuffs, also bound them together. In addition, Solomon and Hiram jointly sponsored trade ventures that took ships representing Israel as far as India! This system of alliance and trade treaties was the key to Solomon's successful foreign relations program.

Economic conditions. Solomon was as aggressive economically as his father had been militarily. He invested in land and sea trade. He developed Is-

155

rael's natural resources, setting up smelteries which excavation has shown brilliantly used prevailing winds to intensify the heat of the furnaces in which metals were refined. Solomon maintained a large court as well as a large army and built many public buildings. He also built the Temple of the Lord which his father had dreamed of: a Temple which cost billions. While Solomon's sources of income were constantly being developed, his expenses still outgrew them; we're told that at one time he borrowed heavily from Hiram.

Solomon drew income from four major sources:

■ Taxation. The country was divided into 12 districts (not along the old tribal lines), and the chief officer over each was primarily a tax collector. The bureaucratic demands grew so heavy that at Solomon's death the people cried out desperately for tax relief (I Ki. 12: 3, 4).

■ Trade. Solomon's ships and caravans traveled to Africa, Arabia, and India, trading copper from his mines for many goods. He also became a middleman in selling military hardware, buying and selling chariots and horses for people to the north and south of Israel.

■ Labor conscriptions. Solomon drafted laborers for his public works projects. At first, the laborers were drawn from the foreign populations over which Israel ruled. Later, when more men were needed, he pressed Israelites into service as well. As such conscripts were expected to work for the government without pay, this was deeply resented.

■ Income was also received from foreign countries. Some of this was annual tribute from subject states, while some gifts were from governments wishing to remain on good terms with powerful Israel.

During Solomon's days Jerusalem became increasingly affluent. The wealth of the world flowed to Solomon's court and was reflected in the glory of the capital city. But bureaucracy grew as well. The nation's wealth was no longer based on the land and what it produced. Increasingly the government controlled the wealth of the land, and taxes drained wealth from the people and funneled expenditure through the central government. The glory was a superficial thing; prosperity was not for the people as much as it was at the expense of the people.

The Temple. Solomon's most massive project was the building of the Temple at Jerusalem. It was located on the site where Abraham had been commanded to sacrifice Isaac (Gen. 22:2). The gold alone used in its construction was worth over two and a half billion dollars (if gold were valued at $35 per ounce). And ten times as much silver as gold had been gathered by David before construction began!

The Temple was similar to the Tabernacle in structure (see *Freedom Road,* ch. 7) but approximately twice as large. Built of stone, paneled over with cedar, and the whole inlaid with gold, the Temple was a strikingly beautiful building. It was fronted by two great pillars, each of which was

FIGURE X

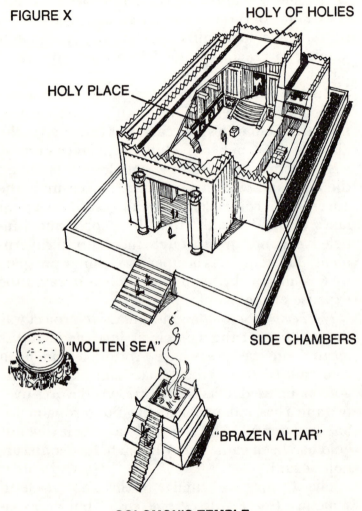

HOLY OF HOLIES

HOLY PLACE

SIDE CHAMBERS

"MOLTEN SEA"

"BRAZEN ALTAR"

SOLOMON'S TEMPLE

topped with a flaming light at night to symbolize the mountaintop presence of Israel's God.

SOLOMON THE MAN

Scripture and archaeology combine to provide an impressive portrait of Solomon's kingdom and his many accomplishments. Three sources give us insight into Solomon the man during the early years of his brilliant reign.

Solomon's prayer (I Ki. 3:3-14). Early in Solomon's rule he was noted for his love for the Lord and his commitment to the Law. He "followed all of his father David's instructions" (3: 3, TLB). On one occasion after a great sacrifice had been made to the Lord, God spoke to Solomon in a dream and told him to make a request. Solomon's response was not only an affirmation of trust in God, but it was also an expression of sensitivity to the significance of his call as king. "And now, O Lord my God, thou hast made thy servant king in place of David my father, although I am but a little child," Solomon humbly said. "I do not know how to go out or come in . . . . Give thy servant therefore an understanding mind to govern thy people, that I may discern between good and evil; for who is able to govern this thy great people?" (I Ki. 3: 7-9, RSV).

This unselfish request was pleasing to God, and was granted: "Behold," God said, "I give you a wise and discerning mind, so that none like you has been before you and none like you shall arise

159

after you" (3:12, RSV). In addition, God promised glory and honor for which Solomon had not asked: "such wealth and honour as no king of your time can match" (3:13, NEB).

The foundation for Solomon's later successes was laid here in his early meeting with God and in the love for God and his people which led Solomon to seek wisdom to govern as God's regent.

Solomon's Temple dedication (I Ki. 8:1–9:9; II Chr. 5–7). Solomon called a great feast for all Israel when the Temple was completed and ready for dedication. After a brief sermon to the people (II Chr. 6:1-11), Solomon faced away from the multitude and knelt down to address God. Calling on God as a covenant-keeping person, Solomon rehearsed some of the promises God had given His people, speaking both of God's commitment to discipline Israel when she sinned and to forgive and restore when Israel returned to God. Calling on the Lord, Solomon asked that God's special presence might be focused in the now completed Temple.

And the Bible tells us, "When Solomon had ended his prayer, fire came down from heaven and consumed the burnt offering and the sacrifices, and the glory of the Lord filled the temple. And the priests could not enter the house of the Lord, because the glory of the Lord filled the Lord's house. When all the children of Israel saw the fire come down and the glory of the Lord upon the temple, they bowed down with their faces to the earth on the pavement, and worshiped and gave thanks to the Lord" (II Chr. 7:1-3, RSV).

In this setting, too, we see Solomon in an excellent light, guiding his people in personal and national dedication to God. God has made Solomon wise, and his wisdom has been used to lead the nation closer to God.

Literary achievements. A third source of insight into the first two decades of Solomon's rule is found in one of his great literary projects: the Book of Proverbs. The Bible tells us that Solomon wrote or collected over three thousand of these practical sayings which sum up the Hebrew people's insights into life. Solomon's literary talents extended beyond this particular form; Ecclesiastes is a treatise in philosophy which sounds a note echoed by many moderns. The Song of Solomon is a love poem showing a distinctive structure and depth. But it is the Proverbs themselves which give us the best insights into Solomon's personal commitment and his character during the first twenty or so years of his reign. It is Proverbs which gives us many insights into ourselves as well.

THE PROVERBS

All Scripture is given to us by God's inspiration (II Tim. 3:16). But not all Scripture has the same purpose, and different literary forms are to be interpreted differently. For instance, a passage like Ephesians 1 gives specific and direct teaching about relationships between the persons of the

161

Godhead and the part of each in redemption. A psalm like Psalm 2 looks into David's experience and shows us how trust in God enabled him to rest in time of great stress. A passage like Joshua 5—6 gives a narrative account of historical events, reporting to us how God worked in a specific space-time situation in the past. Each of these literary forms is different; each has a different purpose and value and use. To affirm that each is inspired by God tells us that the Holy Spirit superintended the writing and recording so that what is communicated to us is both reliable and relevant. We have in words the message God intended us to have, and that message will have meaning for our lives.

But we need to remember that different literary forms are designed to communicate different messages, especially when we come to the Book of Proverbs. For these proverbs, as all proverbs, have characteristics of their own which we need to understand when we interpret and apply them.

Characteristics. What are some of the distinctive characteristics of the proverbs? Commentators list these:

1. The pithy sayings recorded here *express* general truths; they do not attempt to *explain* them. The *how* and *why* simply are not in view. Likewise, the proverbs do not argue. They give no closely reasoned defense of their position. Instead, they simply assume that the reader will see the point and agree.

2. Proverbs has a universalistic rather than par-

162

ticularistic application. Nowhere does the term *Is-rael* appear. Unlike the Law, which was spoken to Israel, these sayings are viewed as relevant to all people of all times. The general principles expressed are universally valid.

3. The outlook in the Book of Proverbs is comprehensive. These sayings probe all of human life and relationships.

4. It is important to realize that the proverbs are generalizations. That is, they express the normal course of events. Like other general principles, they do have exceptions. The New Testament speaks in similar terms: I Peter 3:13, 14 talks about the normal course of events involving positive results for the person who does good. But sometimes a person who does the right thing will suffer for it. In this unusual circumstance, Peter says the believer is to trust God to have a purpose in the unusual events. And Peter gives an example. Jesus, who did right, suffered on a cross. This was not the unjust suffering; it was the just! And what a purpose was in view! Jesus' suffering was for us—and because of His cross you and I have been delivered from death and given eternal life.

Proverbs, then, does not deal with the special events of life, but with the normal. We need to read Proverbs for insight into the way things usually work out in human experience.

5. It is rather striking that the Book of Proverbs, dealing with such a broad range of subjects, does not include any "unscientific" statements. For instance, Proverbs 6: 6-8 accurately describes the so-

163

cial structure of the ant—something that shows acute insight and observation.

6. Unlike other proverbs in the Orient, Proverbs shows a distinctive and high morality. Proverbs gathered by archaeologists from other sources indicate that the sayings of nearby peoples tended to focus on sex and to treat it grossly.

The first four of these often-noted characteristics help us to understand and interpret the Book of Proverbs itself. Studied in this context, the book becomes a very practical and helpful guide to thinking about the life issues which many of us face. The last two characteristics help us very much in understanding Solomon, the chief writer. He remained, for all his marriages, a moral man who, during most of his reign at any rate, was not obsessed with sex. He also was a careful scientific observer, a man whose research, even while ruling a nation, surpassed that of Aristotle. Scripture tells us that Solomon "was the author of 3,000 proverbs and wrote 1,005 songs. He was a great naturalist, with interest in animals, birds, snakes, fish, and trees—from the great cedars of Lebanon down to the tiny hyssop which grows in cracks in the wall. And kings from many lands sent their ambassadors to him for his advice" (I Ki. 4: 32-34, TLB).

Content. The Book of Proverbs has been broken down into from four to ten sections by different commentators, revealing that, like Psalms, this collection is not clearly organized by content or progression of thought. However, two major divisions are very plain. The first nine chapters are a discussion of wisdom, with wisdom often personified.

Chapters 10—31 include several collections of proverbs which involve application of this wisdom to many life situations. As one commentator has suggested, this section contains the "philosophy of the practical life." *The Zondervan Pictorial Encyclopedia of the Bible* gives a number of groupings of the proverbs by topics. They show the range of subjects covered in this small book and also those which are suggested for our own personal Bible study.

The contents of Proverbs can be grouped according to topics discussed, for example, social evils (22:28; 23:10; 30:14); social obligations (18:24; 22:24, 25; 23:1, 2; 25:6, 7, 17; 27:6, 10); poverty (17:5; 18:23; 19:4, 7, 17); concern for the poor (14:31; 17:5, 19; 18:23; 19:7, 17; 21:13; 22:2, 28; 23:10; 30:14); laziness (12:27; 20:13; 26:14, 15); wealth as secondary (11:4; 15:16; 16:8, 16; 19:1; 22:1), but important (10:22; 13:11; 19:4).

Domestic life is a frequent topic (18:22; 21:9, 19; 27:15, 16; 31:30); relationships between parents and children are discussed (10:1; 17:21, 25; 19:1, 26; 20:7; 23:24, 25); the importance of friendship is stressed (18:24; 22:24, 25; 25:17).

No less than four types of fools can be discerned in Proverbs: (1) the simple fool who is still teachable (1:4, 22; 7:7, 8; 21:11); (2) the hardened fool (1:7; 10:23; 12:23; 17:10; 20:3; 27:22) who is obstinate; (3) the arrogant fool, the scoffer who

165

rejects all attempts at enlightment (3: 34; 21: 24; 22: 10; 29: 8); (4) the brutish fool who is "a churl dead to all decency and order" (17: 21; 26: 3; 30: 22; cf. Ps. 14: 1).

Royal conduct is a topic (16: 12-14; 19: 6; 21: 1; 25: 5; 28: 15; 29: 14). Cheerfulness is enjoined (15: 13-15; 17: 22; 18: 14). The use of the tongue is discussed (10: 20; 15: 1; 16: 28; 21: 23; 26: 4). Other personal habits are mentioned (11: 22; 13: 7; 22: 3; 25: 14; 26: 12; 30: 33). Finally some aspects of the concept of life are discussed—its fountain (10: 11; 13: 14; 14: 27; 16: 22); its path (6: 23; 10: 17; 15: 24); and life itself (11: 30; 12: 28; 13: 4, 12). This far-ranging book, then, is a source of many insights which God chose to share with us through His sacred Word.

Uses today. How can we use the Book of Proverbs today? What are its values? In the first place, the concept of wisdom which it explores (Prov. 1—9) and then illustrates (Prov. 10—31) is an important one for moderns. In Proverbs wisdom is not associated so much with knowledge as with choice. The wise person is the one who elects to do good and to turn away from evil. The contemporary idea that we must experience something to know whether it is good for us or bad for us is totally foreign to the spirit of Proverbs. In fact, every human culture has some knowledge of good; all have moral standards and values. The Christian even has revealed moral standards and values, and to some extent knows them. Thus the issue for every man shifts from knowing to choosing. It is here that the wise man and the fool are distinguished. The wise man will choose the good which he knows; the fool will choose the evil. Shifting the emphasis in our culture from knowing to choosing is a particularly important task for our generation, one which a study of Proverbs may encourage.

The topics Proverbs covers are also topics of concern in every society. Today values clarification technology is often applied to help youth and adults discover the values on which they operate. The Book of Proverbs can be applied by Christians concerned with clarifying their values—and learning how to operate on God's.

For individual and for group study, Proverbs remains one of the least explored but richest heritages in the Old Testament—as well as a source of insight into one of history's most remarkable men, Solomon.

GOING DEEPER
to personalize

1. Read II Chronicles 1—9 quickly for a picture of Solomon's time and glory.

2. Study thoroughly the account of the dedication of Solomon's Temple (II Chr. 5—7). Do a detailed analysis of Solomon's prayer (6:12-42). First underline phrases and concepts which you feel are particularly important. Then on a separate sheet of paper jot down *why* you see each underlined item as significant. Finally, in a few paragraphs summarize how what you have noted

in Solomon's prayer has relevance to you in your own relationship with God.

3. Proverbs 22: 6 (RSV) says, "Train up a child in the way he should go, and when he is old he will not depart from it." How does an understanding of the *characteristics* of the proverbs (pp. 162-64) help you to understand this saying? What misunderstandings does it help you avoid? Think of at least three situations in which knowing the characteristics of the proverbs might help you to avoid wrong actions or attitudes based on taking Proverbs 22: 6 as a "promise."

4. Select at least one topic to explore from the topics listed on pages 165, 166. Read the proverbs listed in the text, and from them write a summary paragraph expressing their viewpoint on the topic.

to probe

1. Explore archaeological and other sources to get a complete picture of the era of Solomon.

2. In an earlier chapter it was noted that I and II Chronicles are a commentary with a different perspective than I and II Samuel and I and II Kings, though they all cover, in part, the same periods of Israel's history.

Follow up on this idea, and carefully compare the accounts of Solomon's life and ministry found in I Kings and II Chronicles. What difference do you observe? Write down your discoveries, sharing what you believe God wants us to learn from the special emphases in II Chronicles and specifi-

YEARS OF DARKNESS, DAYS OF GLORY

cally noting how those emphases are of value to
you.

3. From Proverbs 1—9, write at least five pages
discussing and attempting to define the Hebrew
(Biblical) concept of wisdom.

When you have finished, check Hebrew and
Greek lexicons to see if the words translated "wisdom" in both Testaments reinforce or differ from
the definition you developed in your study of
Proverbs in English.

ON THE EDGE OF DARKNESS

IT'S APPROPRIATE that the Chronicles account of Solomon's life leaves out the events recorded in I Kings 11. Scripture affirms that God accepts the believer on the basis of his faith, not his works. Trust frees God to forgive our sin. Both Old and New Testaments open our eyes to the amazing extent and nature of forgiveness. "Their sins and iniquities will I remember no more," says Hebrews 10: 17, echoing Jeremiah 31: 34. Now, in Chronicles, we see this principle in practice. History records that "when Solomon was old his wives turned away his heart after other gods; and his heart was not wholly true to the Lord his God" (I Ki. 11: 4, RSV). But the divine commentary on Solomon concludes with the account of his glory. The years of failure and decline are overlooked.

In this, the Chronicles are something like Hebrews 11, in which God catalogs the accomplishments of men and women of faith. Reading their history in the Old Testament, we are often confronted by their weaknesses and failures—failures we dare not try to explain away. It's wrong to idealize Biblical characters or to excuse their faults, or marshal our "scholarship" to show that things they did were not so bad after all. But it is just as wrong to fail to recognize the fact that in forgiveness God faces sin, deals with it, and sends it to oblivion.

Solomon, like other Old Testament men of faith, trusted a God willing to send His Son to Calvary to deal decisively and eternally with human sin. In the blood of Christ, the unique answer to the fact of sin—yours and mine as well as Solomon's—has been made. God Himself paid sin's penalty in full. Now God exercises the freedom Christ won for Him as well as for us. He accepts trust as the righteousness which we do not have. As for sin, God forgives.

Solomon, then, on the one hand stands before us as an example of the forgiven man. On the other hand, he stands as an example of a man who chose a road on which he remained in constant *need* of forgiveness!

David is an example of the forgiven man as well. David sinned, was called to account, and was restored to fellowship. The wrong directions he took were turned again and again to the way of righteousness. Because David confessed recognized sin, his life with God was essentially one of continual fellowship. Solomon, on the other hand, took a direction from which there is no record that he turned. Because Solomon's relationship with God was founded on initial trust, as his early prayers clearly show, the forgiveness later won on Calvary was his. But because Solomon failed to confess, he wandered from the Lord and lived the last decades of his life out of fellowship.

What we learn from Solomon's life is that sin's impact on the individual and on others around him is utterly tragic. The basic relationship with God may not be broken by later acts of sin. Forgiveness may wash the empty years out of memory. But the contemporary loss in terms of human suffering is tragically great. The fantastic potential of a life completely given to God is lost. The person we could have become by denying our own passions or understanding in order to follow Him dissolves into a sigh.

SOLOMON'S STRENGTH

A simple New Testament warning helps us understand Solomon—and ourselves. "If you think you are standing firm, be careful that you don't fall" (I Cor. 10:12, NIV). We can never retreat from dependence on God. Those very strengths of personality or character that are ours are at the same time the weaknesses through which we will be attacked. Solomon's great strength was his wisdom. Solomon's wisdom was also his weakness.

Solomon's diplomatic policies give clear examples. It certainly seemed wise to make alliances with surrounding countries and to seal those alliances in the normal way with marriages. It also seemed wise to set up the mobile strike force of chariots, which was a keystone in Solomon's military defense. Yet both these "wise" courses of action are warned against in Deuteronomy, the fifth book of Moses. Telling Israel that they might set a king over them when they came into the land, Moses warned against choosing a foreigner. Then he added, "He must not multiply horses for himself, or cause the people to return to Egypt in order to multiply horses . . . . And he shall not multiply wives for himself, lest his heart turn away; nor shall he greatly multiply for himself silver and gold" (Deut. 17:16, 17, RSV).

David had followed these injunctions. While he had several wives and concubines, there was nothing of the multiplication of Solomon (700 wives and 300 concubines!). David also established a policy of incapacitating the chariot horses of the armies he had defeated so they could never be used for war; he had carefully refrained from building up a chariot-based military establishment for himself.

Solomon reasoned that each of these policies was prudent. He apparently failed to see the danger inherent in each course—danger first that foreign wives might entice his heart from following God, and then that becoming a military superpower might lead him to trust his strength rather than his God!

Solomon trusted his wisdom. Why not? His wisdom was renowned. God's warnings were apparently unrealistic. Wisdom dictated a different course from the one commanded by God.

First Kings 11 tells us that God knows human strengths and weaknesses far better than any wise man. In Solomon's old age the women he loved did turn his heart away from the Lord toward their gods. Solomon brought into the holy city itself the worship of the very gods and goddesses which the Lord had commanded to be purged from the land.

Because of this, God announced judgment on Solomon. "And the Lord was angry with Solomon, because his heart had turned away from the Lord, the God of Israel, who had appeared to him twice, and had commanded him concerning this thing, that he should not go after other gods; but he did not keep what the Lord commanded. Therefore the Lord said to Solomon, 'Since this has been your mind and you have not kept my covenant and my statutes which I have commanded you, I will surely tear the kingdom from you and will give it to your servant. Yet for the sake of David your father I will not do it in your days, but I will tear it out of the hand of your son. However I will not tear away all the kingdom; but I will give one tribe to your son, for the sake of David my servant and for the sake of Jerusalem which I have chosen'" (I Ki. 11: 9-13, RSV).

Solomon's failure to trust God rather than his own wisdom was destined to have a tragic impact on the people he led as well as on himself. No human trait, no matter how finely tuned, can function well apart from a relationship with God where that trait is fully submitted and committed. Solomon's wisdom, apart from God's special touch, led him in paths which "seem right to a man" but which led inexorably to death. It is the same for us. However great our strengths, when we rely on them rather than on God we're sure to fall. Charles Pfeiffer comments, "After a 40-year reign the king who is esteemed the wisest of men died, leaving his country on the verge of bankruptcy. He had wonderful opportunities and wonderful accomplishments, but his defection tended to nullify much of his good beginning."

We can trace the impact of Solomon's defection in the events immediately following his death. The nation was split, and enemies made by Solomon's harsh policies, like Hadad the Edomite, attacked the divided kingdom from without. The wealth gathered by Solomon to Jerusalem created oppressed and oppressor classes within. The nation was wealthy, but many people lived in poverty.

It is never easy to discern from such facts what a person's defection from God does with him. Outward things can be measured; the inner spirit must be personally revealed.

This is why the Book of Ecclesiastes is so valuable. David, the emotional man, shared his feelings with us in the Psalms. Solomon, the intellectual man, now shares his inmost thoughts. In fellowship, Solomon shared Spirit-directed wisdom, such as:

176

Trust in the Lord with all your heart,
and do not rely on your own insight.
In all your ways acknowledge him,
and he will make straight your paths.
Proverbs 3:5, 6 (RSV)

When Solomon was out of fellowship during the later years of his rule, he wrote again; but his thinking was different then. During those years Solomon chose to reason out the meaning of life from the data available within the physical universe. It is this reasoning, this exploration of the world in which man lives by reason alone, which we have in Ecclesiastes.

ECCLESIASTES

In the last chapter it was noted that different kinds of Biblical literature must be understood within the framework of their purpose and form. Poetic expression, for instance, should not be taken in exactly the same way as carefully reasoned teaching paragraphs from some New Testament epistle. In order to understand any passage of Scripture, it is important to carefully define its purpose and frame of reference. We need to remember this when we approach the Book of Ecclesiastes.

Ecclesiastes is different from any other book of the Bible. While it is included generally in the category of "wisdom literature" (Job, Proverbs, and Ecclesiastes are examples of this genre), nevertheless, it is still unique. Wisdom literature is

177

universal in its scope; it does not dwell on the Covenant, the election of Israel, redemption, prophecy, sacred history, or Temple. Its focus is on man the creature, his life on earth, and the inscrutability of God and His ways. Ecclesiastes goes beyond this to emphasize the absurdity and futility of human life and knowledge as ends in themselves.

Key phrases. There are three key phrases which help us understand Ecclesiastes:

(1) Twenty-nine times the writer uses the phrase "under the sun" to define the limits he has chosen for his searching. Only data which the senses can test and probe will be considered. Nothing from beyond this space-time universe will be considered. Nowhere in Ecclesiastes is Moses or Scripture or any form of revelation mentioned. Verse 13 of chapter 1 (RSV) illustrates the limits Solomon has set for himself: "I applied my mind to seek and to search out by wisdom all that is done under heaven."

(2) The second key phrase appears seven times and reflects the same limitations; Solomon says that he "communed with my own heart" to reach his conclusions. His methodology is empirical, but all the data he gathers is evaluated by the standard of his own intelligence. In this book Solomon recognizes no higher wisdom than his own; he never looks beyond the conclusions unaided intelligence can make.

(3) The third key word appears 34 times. It is "vanity," more accurately translated "emptiness."

Solomon's determined effort to make sense of human life leads him to the same tragic conclusion of many modern philosophers. Life is absurd. There is no meaning or purpose in human experience. There may be fleeting joys, but ultimately, above the doorway through which men are born into this world and the doorway through which they exit is written, "Vanity of vanities! All is vanity." To paraphrase it:

> Emptiness, emptiness . . .
> All is emptiness.
> Nothing has meaning.

This is not the overall witness of Scripture. God looks beyond the short span of our years of life on earth, and He sees us as we truly are. Created in His image, touched by the eternal, each of us has a destiny that extends far beyond time itself. In light of that heritage from Him and that destiny with Him, existence *does* have meaning.

But Solomon is here looking for meaning within time—and, in fact, within man's lifetime! Using the intelligence with which God has gifted him, Solomon extends his great powers to the limit. But Solomon can find no satisfying purpose for life within the limits he has set. Within these limits life *does* become absurd and each human being loses the possibility of fulfillment.

Interpreting Ecclesiastes. When we know the context in which this book of Scripture was written, we are immediately warned not to draw doctrine from Ecclesiastes as we would from, say, one of Paul's epistles. What is recorded here is Solomon's reasoning; it is not necessarily the divine viewpoint. How then do we interpret this book of the Bible?

(1) *View it as written from the standpoint of human reasoning.* Remember that the book communicates what Solomon thinks rather than what God reveals. As such, it may contain much truth. But the conclusions Solomon reaches do not necessarily express God's own thoughts or will.

(2) *Remember that inspiration in this case means that Solomon's reasoning is accurately recorded.* Inspiration does not guarantee that everything recorded is truth.

(3) *Compare problem passages with the whole of God's revelation.* Where a conclusion or insight seems questionable, it is important to compare it with the rest of Scripture. In most other passages God is revealing *His* thoughts through men.

Taken in this way, Ecclesiastes gives us a penetrating insight into Solomon himself as well as into all those many, many wise men since his day who have yearned to understand life, but who have searched for meaning apart from God and found only despair.

SONG OF SOLOMON

There is another Old Testament book written by Solomon: The Song of Solomon. In this book, a

180

love poem, Solomon is not engaged in some speculative search for life's meaning, but simply in the enjoyment by lovers of each other.

The book has raised a great deal of speculation through the ages, some believing that there is a deeper meaning underlying the love poem. Three approaches to its interpretation are:

1. The allegorical. The poem is seen to represent God's love for Israel.

2. The typical. The events are historical, but intended as a type (a foreshadowing) of the relationship between Christ and the Church.

3. The literal. The book simply portrays the beauty of love between man and woman—courtship, marriage, and married love. In this view, the basic message is affirmation of the beauty and purity of love and marriage.

The third view was held in the early church and is still held by many today. Dr. J. Vernon McGee in his commentary summarizes the plot of the Song of Solomon this way:

The key to the story is found in (8:11) and tells of a poor family in Ephraim in which there was a girl who was a sort of Cinderella. The poverty of the family forced her into the vineyards where she meets the young shepherd. The story of their love is first told. Then he leaves her with the promise that he will return. He is absent a long time, and she despairs of his return. One day the electrifying word is shouted along the way that King Solomon is coming by. She is not interested and takes no notice until word is brought that King Solomon wants to see her. She is puzzled until she is brought into his presence where she recognizes him as her shepherd lover. He takes her to his palace in Jerusalem where most of the song takes place. It is a drama, and it has the daughters of Jerusalem who carry along the tempo of the story. Several lovely scenes are introduced at Jerusalem which find counterpart in the church.

McGee passes on this interesting information as well:

The Jews called it the Holy of Holies of Scripture. Origin and Jerome tell us that the Jews would not permit their young men to read it until they were thirty years old. Also, it was commonly read at the time of passover, and seemed to picture to the Jews the love of Jehovah for Israel.

SOLOMON: AN EVALUATION

With the Solomonic era the kingdom of Israel reached a peak unattained before or since. Nations feared and honored Israel and her king, whose wealth and wisdom, even today, are bywords in the East.

As usual, the world's evaluation of Solomon and his leadership shows a superficial understanding of the issues of life. Solomon brought wealth and power to Israel, but wealth and power did not bring meaning either to his people or to Solomon himself. The bureaucracy Solomon built brought his rich and powerful land to the edge of bankruptcy!

As a man, Solomon started well, with a deep commitment to God. But Solomon's strength—his wisdom—also proved to be his weakness. He began to rely on his intelligence and his own wisdom rather than God's. As a result, his own spiritual life became deadened as his wives turned his heart from the Lord. During the last years of his life, this man, who had written of wisdom and had distilled meaningful insights about life into thousands of proverbs, turned away from God. He attempted to find life's meaning while ruling God out—and found only deepening despair and disillusionment.

Solomon had every opportunity to test all those ways in which men today search for fulfillment. He probed the possibilities of the intellectual life. He abandoned himself to pleasure and luxury. He gathered great wealth and built great buildings and public works. He experienced an exciting and varied sexual life. He had power and status within and outside his kingdom. Yet all these things when tasted seemed flat and meaningless. None could give his life meaning.

Even his final sayings in Ecclesiastes 12 do not represent a return to God. They represent the best thinking of the natural man. Perhaps there *is* a

183

God. If so, what more can man do than keep His commandments? Possibly chapter 12 reflects a wistful look back on Solomon's own life when he did fear God and keep His commandments before the evil days came, and years drew on, when Solomon looked at all his glory and accomplishments and realized, "I have no pleasure in them" (Eccl. 12: 1, RSV).

And so Solomon died.

In his death Solomon, like all the men whose lives are preserved on the pages of God's Word, left us a heritage.

Solomon left us a warning that our strengths may be our weaknesses too. Solomon left us a warning that beginning life well is only half of it. And Solomon left us a message. The purposes of God could not be fulfilled in the ideal worldly environment that was Israel's Camelot. God has something more in mind for His people than place and power in the family of nations. The secret of God's purpose for Israel—and of His purpose for you and me—can be found only in a deep and close personal relationship with Him. It is the presence of God—not the presence of Solomon's gold—that is the true glory of God's people.

The glory that was Israel's in Solomon's time has faded now. Nothing remains. But the glory that will be Israel's when Jesus, David's greater Son, sits on the throne—the glory that will be ours with Him—is still ahead.

In that eternal Kingdom, the ultimate glory will be known.

GOING DEEPER
to personalize

1. Read I Kings 11. How do you explain the decline of Solomon's kingdom? Do you see trends in your own country that are similar?

2. It is very important to understand the inner man when we think about Solomon's last years. Read quickly through Ecclesiastes, and write down three or four "feeling words" that sum up the tone of the book.

3. Read through Ecclesiastes carefully, listing those ways in which Solomon tried to find meaning for his life. List also why each way fell short of providing what Solomon sought.

4. Sum up your own personal philosophy of life in a few paragraphs. Where do *you* expect to find meaning? How have you done in your search so far?

to probe

1. There are other views than the author's about Ecclesiastes, its meaning and purpose. Review the arguments and the evidence and write a short paper giving your personal conclusions.

2. Do research in several theology books on the doctrine of inspiration. What is the relationship between inspiration and truth? Inspiration and revelation?

THE COURSE OF EVENTS

THE BIBLE GIVES THE HISTORY of the human race—past and future. We could have never known about Creation or redemption or all the other facts of sacred history unless they had been revealed to us in God's written Word, the Bible (I Cor. 2: 9-13).

Through the Bible we learn that history has a definite beginning and an end. There is a direction to history; it moves toward a goal set for the human race as well as for the individual. It is in the Old Testament that we sense most clearly this definite goal. Here the plan of history is defined, and here we are privileged to see it working out. And as we trace the outworking of God's plan, we hear and find messages directed to us now. And we are able to put each historical purpose in an overall perspective.

PHASE I: CREATION

Genesis 1 and 2 provide the context. We come to understand the universe we live in and our place in it. The Bible tells us that God created the material universe from nothing, and all that exists must be understood in the personal framework that God Himself provides. The universe is not an impersonal "thing," but, rather, the planned expression of God's might and power and personality.

Genesis also explains man as being the focus and pinnacle of Creation—a creature made in the image of God and thereby vested with significance and a derived glory. Man cannot be understood unless he is seen as irrevocably related to the eternal, though temporarily occupying space and time. Because man is made in God's image, each individual is of vital importance to God and special to Him.

So these earliest chapters of Scripture introduce us to ourselves and define our identity. They explain why each of us stands in need of a vital relationship with God. Without such a relationship to the God whose image we bear, each of us is incomplete. God made us for Himself, and we are restless and ill at ease apart from Him.

PHASE II: SIN

The Biblical account moves beyond the initial Creation and, in Genesis 3, shares the story of Adam's fall. This report accounts for the alienation and loneliness we each feel, as well as for the tugging power of sin to which we are each subject. In Adam, mankind chose to attempt life apart from God. Adam traded trust in His Creator for the empty privilege of choosing to do wrong. Ever since then, society and individuals have shown the agonizing warp of sin-sick personalities.

When Adam sinned, something vital in each person's life died. Death, not life, became the experience of all men.

PHASE III: SIN'S OUTCOME IN ADAM'S FAMILY

Chapters 4 and 5 of Genesis examine the impact of sin. In Adam's own family, we see one son murder his brother and go on to establish a civilization in which harming others becomes a way of life.

Already in history events had begun to demonstrate the reality and awfulness of sin. Satan had denied that sin led to death; now man would drink deeply of all that death really means—the dissolution of the personality and the return of the body to the dust.

God acted to cover Adam and Eve's sin. God had already introduced the idea of sacrifice. But since Adam had chosen sin, the ultimate meaning of this pathway would now become known. Adam had refused to trust; now God would demonstrate across the centuries and millenniums of human history how utterly true His words and warnings are.

PHASE IV: SIN'S OUTCOME IN JUDGMENT

As the race multiplied and spread across the earth, the expressions of sin we read of in Genesis 4 and 5 multiplied. When "every imagination of the thoughts of [man's] heart was only evil continually" (Gen. 6: 5, RSV), God acted to bring the judgment of the Flood on the human race (Gen. 6—9). This cataclysm communicated the fact that sin not only twists human life, but it also incurs guilt. And guilt forces a holy God to judge.

One family, Noah's, was borne over the waters and planted in a renewed world. Mankind was given a fresh start by a man who had enough faith in God to obey His instructions to build a boat.

PHASE V: HISTORY REPEATS ITSELF

Genesis 10 and 11 pick up the history of the race after the Flood. Again man disobeyed God. Rather than scattering to accept God-given dominion over creation (see Gen. 1: 28), the postdiluvian people attempted to build a society without Him. So God scattered them Himself, confusing their language.

It was probably at the very end of this period, around the time of Abraham, that Job lived. A godly man in an ungodly culture, Job illustrated early faith in God—and the loss of knowledge of God which came as the generations passed. God still cares for and deals with individuals, but sin has twisted the course of the race into unfruitful paths.

PHASE VI: ABRAHAM'S CALL

With the introduction of Abram in Genesis 12, history took a new direction. God spoke to this pagan from Ur, and Abram responded. To Abram, God gave a series of great promises in a Covenant expressed in Genesis 12, 15, and 17. God announced the course of history ahead of time, as well as the purpose He would fulfill as history moved toward its intended culmination.

God announced that He would no longer work with the race as a whole but would work *for* all mankind through Abraham's (Abram's name was changed to Abraham as a token of fulfillment) descendants. To these descendants God promised a specific land, great blessings, and a special relationship with Him. He also promised that through this people would come one in whom the whole human race would be blessed.

From that time on, Abraham, his children, and his grandchildren began to look at themselves and be seen as God's chosen people. God's purposes in history are to be worked out through them. These people are the key to understanding the past and the future: what has been, and what must surely be.

PHASE VII: CAPTIVITY IN EGYPT

After three generations, Abraham's descendants moved from Palestine, the land of the Covenant promise, to Egypt. There the people of Israel

191

(named for Abraham's grandson Jacob, who had been renamed Israel by God), waited for the next step in God's plan to unfold.

At first the Israelites were guests in Egypt. Then a series of political changes transformed their status and they became slaves. As slaves, God's people suffered under harsh taskmasters. Because they multiplied so quickly, the Egyptians even initiated a policy of killing their male children when they were born.

Israel remembered the old stories of a God who spoke to their forefathers and made great promises. But under the harsh reality of their immediate circumstances, the past they recalled and the future they dreamed of must have seemed tragically unreal.

Over generations of slavery, the people of Israel were humbled and crushed. They discovered through suffering that there was no inherent strength in themselves that could win them freedom. Release could only come through the intervention of God.

PHASE VIII: DELIVERANCE

God did intervene. Exodus tells us how God sent Moses to confront Pharaoh, Egypt's ruler. God's first demands that Pharaoh let His people go were refused. This brought a series of terrible judgments on the Egyptian people. Finally God struck down the oldest son in each Egyptian family; in terror, the Egyptians thrust Israel out of the land.

The redemption of Israel from Egypt by God's direct and personal intervention is a symbol of all redemption. What man cannot do to free himself from sin's slavery, God can do.

The redemption from Egypt also reaffirmed to Israel the faithfulness of God. God remembered His Covenant with Abraham and acted to keep His promises.

In order that Israel might always remember their need for God's intervention, the Passover feast was instituted. This annual time of remembering deliverance was designed to remind Israel that God was the source of their freedom.

In a series of continuing miracles, including the opening of the Red Sea for Israel and its closing to destroy a pursuing Egyptian army, God demonstrated His firm intention to free His people forever from the slavery under which they had suffered.

PHASE IX: THE LAW

Israel's redemption from Egypt freed them from external tyranny. But events soon demonstrated that they were in bondage to an inner tyranny that was even more destructive. Sin sinks its roots deeply even into the personalities of redeemed men and women. Once out of Egypt, God's people murmured and complained, forgetting His commitment to them, and they began to doubt and resist Moses at every turn.

To set standards which would reveal God's own

character and show the way He expected His people to live, God guided the Israelites to Sinai. There, as told in Exodus 19—24, God gave His people the Mosaic Law. This Law not only established moral standards, but also began to define the distinctive life-style which God was to hold His people to, both for their benefit and as a testimony.

But, again, the Law provided an external standard. It did not change Israel within. The continuing story of the redeemed generation shows their inability to trust God, which led to disobedience. Commanded to enter the Promised Land, Israel refused. The people were condemned to 38 years of wandering in the wilderness until the generation that had known God's deliverance from Egypt died. Because of unbelief they were unable to enter into the promised rest.

PHASE X: THE NEW GENERATION

The men and women who had seen God's mighty acts in Egypt, but had refused to trust Him, died. Their children now stood poised on the edge of the Promised Land. In Deuteronomy, we hear Moses restate the Law and sketch again the life-style of trust to which God called His people. In Joshua we see the new generation respond to God and follow their new leader to victory.

The Promised Land was taken in a series of swift military moves, with God making His presence known on the side of His people at Jericho and in other actions.

With opposition in the land rendered ineffective, the people of God settled into their promised rest.

PHASE XI: SIN APPEARS AGAIN

Even though Israel had now moved into an ideal environment, and a life-style designed by God to bless His people, the ancient specter of sin again reared up. The generations that followed drifted away from God and turned to growing disobedience. Over the decades, the life-style of Israel deteriorated. God judged sin with the removal of the blessing, and Israel's enemies gained ascendancy over the twelve tribes. Yet, when Israel returned to God, He sent deliverers or "judges" to free them from their enemies and lead them into His ways.

The more than 330 years during which the judges ruled were days of continual ups and downs for Israel. But the trend of history was downward. The days of the judges were dark days, days during which sin's dreadful dominion was demonstrated even under that divinely ordained system of government, the theocracy, which was the best man has ever known.

PHASE XII: THE KINGDOM

Israel finally demanded a new system of government, seeking in a transition from a theocracy to a monarchy the freedom from the tendency to drift into social and personal sin.

Israel's first king, Saul, demonstrated once again that the root of the sin problem is in man, not in society. But then God gave Israel a godly king, David. Following God with his whole heart, David led Israel to a foreshadowing of that glory which God had told His people to expect. The kingdom continued to grow in glory under Solomon, David's son. But in the latter half of his reign, Solomon abandoned the God of his father, David, and began to trust his own wisdom—and seek other gods. When Solomon turned away from God, the kingdom he ruled inevitably took directions which meant the ultimate loss of that glory Israel had begun to know.

Once again a fresh start had proven unable to bring the promised blessing of God. Sin had again brought the hopes of men to ruin.

THE LESSON

So far in our journey through Biblical history, we've seen that no changes in external conditions have brought men to the condition of blessedness and dominion God intends for us. Yet, men still struggle to find release and fulfillment without Him, denying God's judgment that sin has brought death, and that death still holds man and society in its unbreakable grip.

Looking ahead, we'll trace in our further studies in the Old Testament God's further revelation of His great solution to man—and society's!—need. And we will see further evidence that nothing apart from this final culminating act of God in Christ can stand as a meaningful hope for the world.

But there is a personal message in the Old Testament as well. It is a message that affirms a basic truth for each individual. The death we see expressed in history and society grips you and me as well. You and I must turn from our own efforts and reject all the tempting solutions the world may offer; we must seek God's intervention in our own life. As the New Testament phrases God's message to the individual, "You were dead in your trespasses and sins, in which you formerly walked" (Eph. 2:1, 2, NASB).

The passage, Ephesians 2, goes on to explain: "But God, being rich in mercy, because of His great love with which He loved us, even when we were dead in our transgressions, made us alive together with Christ" (2:4, 5, NASB).

In the person of Jesus Christ, promised in the Old Testament and revealed in the New, God has acted to bring to you and me the possibility of life and to call us from the experience of sin's death to a new and abundant life with Him.

If we've heard the message of Biblical history, our eyes have been turned away from ourselves and our own efforts to God. If we've heard the message of Biblical history, we have recognized the reality of death, spiritual and physical. If we have heard the message of Biblical history, we can begin to realize that our one and only hope is in God, creator and savior.

GOING DEEPER
to personalize

1. Work through the phases discussed in this chapter and, for each phase, carefully define the "personal message for *me*" that it communicates. That is, what does each of these phases of Old Testament history tell you about your own relationship with God and your way of living?

2. The author organized this chapter and the phases around the dominant theme of death and death's demonstration in human history. Can you think of any other ways to organize (and recapitulate) the same history?

FIGURE XI

Period	Theme	Books
I. PRIMEVAL PERIOD	CREATION Creation to Abraham	*Genesis 1–11* *Job*
II. PATRIARCHAL PERIOD (2166-1446)*	COVENANT Abraham to Moses	*Genesis 12–50*
III. EXODUS PERIOD (1446-1406)	LAW Moses' Leadership	*Exodus* *Numbers* *Leviticus* *Deuteronomy*
IV. CONQUEST OF CANAAN (1406-1390)	CONQUEST Joshua's Leadership	*Joshua*
V. TIME OF JUDGES (1367-1050)	JUDGES No Leadership	*Judges* *Ruth* *I Samuel 1–7*
VI. UNITED KINGDOM (1050-931)	KINGDOM Monarchy Established	*I Samuel 8–31* *II Samuel 1–24* *I Kings 1–11* *I Chronicles* *II Chronicles 1–9*
	Establishment (David)	*Psalms*
	Decline (Solomon)	*Ecclesiastes* *Proverbs* *Song of Solomon*

*The dates are taken from *A Survey of Israel's History* by Leon Wood (Grand Rapids: Zondervan, 1975).

VII. DIVIDED KINGDOM (931-722) Israel Elijah Elisha **Judah**	PROPHETIC MOVEMENT Two Kingdoms	I Kings 12–22 II Kings 1–17 II Chronicles 10–29 Jonah Obadiah Amos Hosea Micah Joel Isaiah
VIII. SURVIVING KINGDOM (722-586)	Judah Remains	II Kings 18–25 II Chronicles 30–36 Jeremiah Nahum Zephaniah Habakkuk
IX. BABYLONIAN CAPTIVITY (586-538)	JUDGMENT Torn from Palestine	Ezekiel Daniel Esther
X. RESTORATION (538-400)	The Jews Return 400 Years Between the Testaments	Ezra Nehemiah Haggai Zechariah Malachi